HUNGER MAKES ME
A MODERN GIRL

HUNGER MAKES ME A MODERN GIRL

A MEMOIR

CARRIE BROWNSTEIN

virago

VIRAGO

First published in the United States in 2015 by Riverhead
First published in Great Britain in 2015 by Virago Press

3 5 7 9 10 8 6 4

A CIP catalogue record for this book
is available from the British Library.

Hardback ISBN 978-0-349-00792-2
Trade paperback ISBN 978-0-349-00793-9

Printed and bound in Great Britain by
Clays Ltd, St Ives plc

Papers used by Virago are from well-managed forests
and other responsible sources.

MIX
Paper from
responsible sources
FSC
www.fsc.org FSC® C104740

Virago Press
An imprint of
Little, Brown Book Group
Carmelite House
50 Victoria Embankment
London EC4Y 0DZ

An Hachette UK Company
www.hachette.co.uk

www.virago.co.uk

For Corin and Janet

CONTENTS

Prologue: 2006   ix

PART 1 // YOUTH

Chapter 1   The Sound of Where You Are   3

Chapter 2   That's Entertainment   11

Chapter 3   Disappearance   27

Chapter 4   No Normal   41

Chapter 5   Born Naked   51

PART 2 // SLEATER-KINNEY

Chapter 6   Schooled   79

Chapter 7   Self-Titled   93

Chapter 8   *Call the Doctor*   103

Chapter 9   Mediated   117

Chapter 10   Hello, Janet   121

Chapter 11   Sellouts   129

Chapter 12   *Dig Me Out*   137

Chapter 13   *The Hot Rock*   153

Chapter 14   Help   159

Chapter 15   *All Hands on the Bad One*   165

Chapter 16   *One Beat*   177

Chapter 17   Opening Up   187

Chapter 18   *The Woods*   199

Chapter 19   Be Still This Sad Year   217

PART 3 // AFTERMATH

Chapter 20   Shelter   225

Chapter 21   Home   237

Epilogue   239

Acknowledgments   243

2006

I only wanted one thing on tour: to slam my hand in a door and break my fingers. Then I would go home.

I had shingles on the right side of my body, brought on by stress, a perfect triangle of blisters that flickered and throbbed with a stinging electricity. At night I could barely sleep from the discomfort, flailing about in a twin bed in a dingy European hotel room while a bandmate dozed a foot away from me. During the day, on the long drives between European cities, I rode in the back of a Sprinter van, pressed against the firm handshake of the seat, rigid and without any give. I watched DVDs of an American television show on my computer, the first season of a drama all about plotting an escape from prison. Occasionally I glanced at my fingers and thought about how hard I'd have to slam the door.

On May 27, my band Sleater-Kinney arrived in Brussels, Belgium, to play a venue called Le Botanique. The shingles virus made me a loner. Janet had never had the chicken pox as a child, and thus I was contagious to her. After Janet checked in with her sister, a doctor in L.A., the term "airborne" entered the conversation. But I already felt liminal and weightless, outside myself, a series of free-floating particles that only occasionally cohered into humanness, into arms and legs. Tour reassembles you; it's a fragmentary and jarring existence even without an added illness or malady. But now I could not find the floor; I was outside the room, outside myself. The three of us hung around backstage before the show: fluorescent lights, a mirror, buckets of ice, a picked-at deli tray. Corin gingerly helped button the back of my shirt, careful not to touch me or get too close. It's okay, I thought, this isn't my body, I'm not here.

The show was about to start and I couldn't feel a thing.

Sleater-Kinney was my family, the longest relationship I had ever been in; it held my secrets, my bones, it was in my veins, it had saved my life countless times, it still loved me even when I was terrible to it, it might have been the first unconditional love I'd ever known.

And I was about to destroy Sleater-Kinney.

PART 1

YOUTH

CHAPTER 1

THE SOUND OF WHERE YOU ARE

I've always felt unclaimed. This is a story of the ways I created a territory, something more than just an archipelago of identities, something that could steady me, somewhere that I belonged.

My story starts with me as a fan. And to be a fan is to know that loving trumps being beloved. All the affection I poured into bands, into films, into actors and musicians, was about me and about my friends. Once, in high school, I went to see the B-52s. I pressed myself against the barrier until bruises darkened my ribs, thrilled to watch Kate Pierson drink from a water bottle, only to have my best friend tell me that to her the concert wasn't about the band—it was about *us*, it was about the fact that we were there together, that the music itself was secondary to our world, merely something that colored it, spoke to it. That's why all those records from high school sound so good. It's not that the songs were better—it's that we were listening to them with our friends, drunk for the first time on liqueurs, touching sweaty palms, staring for hours at a poster on the wall, not grossed out by carpet or dirt or crumpled, oily bedsheets. These songs and albums were the best ones because of how huge adolescence felt then, and how nostalgia recasts it now.

Nostalgia is so certain: the sense of familiarity it instills makes us feel like we know ourselves, like we've lived. To get a sense that we have already journeyed through something—survived it, experienced it—is often so much easier and less messy than the task of currently living through something. Though hard to grasp, nostalgia is elating to bask in—temporarily restoring color to the past. It creates a sense memory that momentarily simulates context. Nostalgia is recall without the criticism of the present day, all the good parts, memory without the pain. Finally, nostalgia asks so little of us, just to be noticed and revisited; it doesn't require the difficult task of negotiation, the heartache and uncertainty that the present does.

Now I can't listen to some of these records alone, in my house that I have cleaned and organized, books arranged just so, sheets washed. The sounds don't hold up. In these cases, fandom is contextual and experiential: it's not that it happened, it's that you were there. It's site-specific, age-specific. Being a fan has to do with the surroundings, and to divorce the sounds from that context often feels distancing, disorienting, but mostly disappointing. I think of all the times I've had a friend over and pulled out records from high school or college, ready for the album to change someone's life the way it changed mine. I watch my friend's face, waiting eagerly for the "aha!" moment to arrive, only to realize that my affection for this intentionally off-key singing, saggy bass sound, and lyrics about bunnies isn't quite the revelation it was fifteen years ago. "You had to be there" is not always a gloat or admonishment—often it's an explanation for why something sounds utterly terrible.

Yet there is much music that survives de- and recontextualization and that needs no experiential reference point. In this case, the role of the fan is still to be a participant, and to participate is to grant yourself permission to immerse, to willingly, gladly, efface and subsume yourself for the sake of the larger meaning but also to provide meaning. It's symbiotic. My favorite kind of musical experience is to feel afterward that your heart is filled up and transformed, like it is pumping a whole new kind of blood into your veins. This is what it is to be a fan: curious, open, desiring for connection, to feel like art has chosen you, claimed you as its witness.

I grew up in the suburbs of Seattle, mostly in Redmond, Washington, a once-rural town that by the late twentieth century was a metonym for Microsoft. Cities frequently deride or deny their outlying residents, thinking them callow; Seattle was my beacon and muse, but it was never really mine. My parents, both raised Jewish in Chicago, were quick to adopt the religion of Christmas, though I should acknowledge the transitional years wherein we awoke to scattered presents under a menorah. Poor Santa, arriving during the night with nothing to choose from but that menorah and a houseplant. Then my mother left when I was fourteen, seeking a cure for herself but leaving another form of sickness and longing behind. It was a childhood of halfways, of in-betweens.

Until I was in high school, every concert I attended was an event, a spectacle. My first was Madonna. She began her *Like a Virgin* tour in Seattle, playing three shows at the Paramount Theatre, with a capacity of less than three thousand. It was 1985, and I was in fifth grade. An agreement was made between my father and my friend's mom. She'd get up at an unkind hour on a Saturday morning so that we could wait in line at Ticketmaster, and my dad would stay out past his bedtime and accompany us to the actual show.

I had my outfit planned. I wanted to wear what any self-respecting female Madonna fan would want to wear in the mid-'80s: a wedding dress. I even asked to borrow my mom's, as if she'd be as flattered as she would have been had I asked to wear it for my real, future wedding. "That's inappropriate," I was told by both my parents, not just in regard to the wedding garment but also in response to my request to wear a crop top with nothing underneath it but a black bra. (I didn't need to wear a bra at the time.) Even fingerless lace gloves were out of the question. I ended up clad in a short-sleeve Esprit button-up covered in pineapples and other exotic fruits, an outfit that did not land me in the local paper that ran a feature on the concert including pictures of fans waiting in line, dressed like Madonna.

By the time the music began, I didn't care that I looked like a cocktail server at a beach resort.

Opening the show was a group of young smart alecks who no one in the Pacific Northwest had ever heard of—they were called the Beastie Boys. We collectively booed them in anticipation of our idol. Then Madonna came out and I remember only two things: she did multiple outfit changes and I screamed the entire time.

When my father and I got home, I couldn't sleep. I kept going in my parents' room to regale my mother with details about what songs Madonna played and how she looked. "She's high," my dad said to my mother, laughing. And I was. It was a moment I'll never forget, a total elation that momentarily erased any outline of darkness. There was light everywhere I looked.

A few years later, in junior high, I saw the *Faith* tour and witnessed George Michael run in tight pants from east to west and back again across the stage. From my seat on the center of the stadium floor, Michael was reduced in size, an action figure. But the experience itself was immense;

the grandiosity was ungraspable, it was the Olympics, it was a mountain, it was outer space. In the middle of the show, my fourteen-year-old friend turned to me and said, "I want to give George Michael a blow job." I was confused. Wasn't I there simply for the songs, to clap my hands and scream, "I want your sex," without actually wanting your sex? But when my friend inserted desire, an actual longing and physical response, into what I thought had been an abstract idea, I had to think about the ways music really made me feel. In that moment, among thousands of people, I *was* light-headed and sweaty. I could not contain a smile; my body was moving in somewhat innocent shimmies but also in shudders, an act that certainly connotes a deeper, reflexive, ecstatic response. I turned away from my friend, nodding in agreement that, yes, the reaction to this music was embodied, was intense. But I also knew in that moment that I would much rather *be* the object of desire than dole it out from the sidelines, or perched on my knees.

Yet the music I was hearing and the concerts I was witnessing were also mystifying and inaccessible. It was the '80s, and much of what I loved was synthed-out pop and Top 40 music, more programmed than played. The music was in the room and in my body, yet I had no idea how it had been assembled or how to break it apart. If I wanted to learn a Madonna song, for example, I'd obtain the piano sheet music and plunk out an anemic version of it on the keys, so wholesome that I was re-virginizing "Like a Virgin" right there in the living room. I practiced David Lee Roth stage moves—well, only one: JUMP—and entered my elementary school talent show as a dancer accompanying a band of sixth-graders playing Ratt's "Round and Round." I remained merely a fan, an after-school bedroom lip-syncher and a family-gathering thanks-for-humoring-me entertainer, with no means of claiming the sounds as my own.

Then I bought my first guitar and saw my first punk and rock shows.
Buying your first guitar in the suburbs does not entail anything
that resembles the folklore. There is not an old bluesman who gifts you
a worn-out, worn-in instrument, with a sweat-and-blood-stained fret-
board, neck dusty from the rails, possessing magic but also a curse.
Rather, you go with your mom or dad to a carpeted store that smells
of antiseptic, where everything is shiny and glistening with newness,
where other parents are renting saxophones or clarinets for their kids
to play in the school jazz band, where some other kid is being publicly
denied a drum kit on account of his parent's sanity. The cheapness,
the vagueness of brands, the generic aspect of it all screams "WARE-
HOUSE FOR THE NONCOMMITTAL." I left with a Canadian-
made solid state amp and a cherry red Epiphone copy of a Stratocaster.
It was the first big purchase I made with my own money. I was fifteen.

In tenth grade, a few of my friends were old enough to drive, and
I started making my way out of the suburbs and into Seattle on the
weekends. Some of the shows we saw were at big venues, like the Moore
or the Paramount Theatre: the Church, the Ramones, Sonic Youth, the
Jesus and Mary Chain. But most of the time, we'd go to smaller places
like the Party Hall or the OK Hotel, and we'd see Northwest-based
bands like Treepeople, Kill Sybil, Hammerbox, Engine Kid, Aspirin
Feast, Galleons Lap, Christ on a Crutch, and Positive Greed.

Here I could get close to the players themselves. I could see how the
drums worked with the guitars and bass, I could watch fingers move
along the frets and feet stomp down on effects pedals, I saw the set lists
taped to the floor, and sometimes I was close enough to see the amp or
pickup settings. I observed the nature of the bands, their internal interactions, their relationships to one another, as much as I listened. It seems
obvious, but it was the first time I realized that music was playable, not

just performable—that it had a process and a seed, a beginning, middle, and end.

Everyone who plays music needs to have a moment that ignites and inspires them, calls them into the world of sound and urges them to make it. And I suppose this form of witness could happen aurally; perhaps it's as easy as hearing an Andy Gill riff or a Kim Gordon cadence and knowing intuitively how that all works. Then you form those sounds yourself, with your own hands and your own voice. Or maybe you see it on a video, in footage of a musician who finally translates and unlocks what you thought was a mystery.

For me, however, I needed to be there—to see guitarists like Kim Warnick and Kurt Bloch of the Fastbacks or Doug Martsch of Treepeople play chords and leads, or Calvin Johnson and Heather Lewis from Beat Happening, in the wholly relatable attire of threadbare T-shirts and jean shorts, enact a weird nerd sexiness, strangely minimal, maximally perverse. I could watch them play songs that weren't coming out of thin air or from behind a curtain. I needed to press myself up against small stages, risking crushed toes, bruised sides, and the unpredictable undulation of the pit, just so I could get a glimpse of who I wanted to be.

CHAPTER 2

THAT'S ENTERTAINMENT

As a child I was engaged in a continuous dialogue with fantasy, escapism, and performance, from conducting mock interviews with the posters and pictures on my bedroom wall (I had so many questions for Madonna, the members of Duran Duran, and Elvis), to attempting to turn the woods behind my house into a restaurant (a task that involved sweeping the forest floor and nailing planks into fallen logs that would serve as tables), to spending hours concocting and recording an outgoing answering machine message that could serve the dual purpose of functionality and an audition, to dressing up as a clown for my sister's birthday in lieu of my parents hiring a real one. I had very little desire to be present, only to be presentational, or to pretend.

I was enamored with the past, the anachronistic. I didn't feel like I was misplaced and in the wrong era, it's just that my obsessions often tilted backward in time. I exalted the old movie stars. I watched black-and-white films on AMC, setting the VCR to record *Dark Victory* with Bette Davis or Preston Sturges's *The Lady Eve*. I collected coffee-table books with Cecil Beaton photographs of Garbo, Marlene Dietrich, Cary Grant, and Gary Cooper. I read Katharine Hepburn's account of

filming *The African Queen* and bought James Dean posters for my wall.
When I was about ten years old, I saw a commercial on TV for a *Time
Life* record collection of doo-wop songs, ordered them COD—cash
on delivery—then hid when the mailman showed up with the package while my mom paid up in order to save face. Any embarrassment I
caused my mother—that she momentarily had to pretend to be a suburban housewife with nothing better to do than order music off the TV
to listen to while she vacuumed—and the subsequent scolding I got
was worth it. Soon I could dance around in the rec room to such out-
of-date hits as "A Little Bit of Soap" and "A Teenager in Love."

I didn't believe the past world was better than my present-day life,
but I connected to—aspired to—the glamour, the iconic images, which
seemed unimpeachable and monolithic. There was a stillness about the
past, a clarity, the way it had been somewhat defined and dissected, in
the rearview mirror; it was there for the taking, for the mining. The old
songs, the old movies, the black-and-white pictures created a visual
and aural time machine. It wasn't that I imagined I had another life—it
was that I didn't have to exist in the here and now. It was a total, freeing effacement.

Yet I was simultaneously trying to forge connections with people
who had a pulse—just not with people whom I actually knew or who
lived anywhere near me. In the '80s, there was a currency to having pen
pals, and the more exotic the location of your pen pal, the better. My
epistolary cache was not geographically impressive. I'd made friends
with some kids at camps with whom I kept in touch, but they merely
lived on the other side of Washington state, or ten minutes away but
went to a different school, which might as well be across the ocean when
you're young and don't have a car. The farthest the mail came for me was
from British Columbia, where a girl I'd met through a soccer exchange

program lived. In comparison, friends of mine were getting letters from exotic, far-flung places like France or Vietnam. They'd bring the thin, light-blue airmail envelopes to school and we'd fawn over the foreign stamps and careful handwriting—*So tiny! Is that how beautiful English could really be?*—the way one would over kittens. A competitive spirit ensued. I thought about what could top a correspondence from Europe or Asia. Why, one from Hollywood, of course.

In the back of the teen magazines I was reading, like *Bop* or *16*, were addresses for all the film and TV stars I loved—not home addresses, of course, more like Ralph Macchio, ^c/o some studio or agency, or a PO box where you could ostensibly reach Ricky Schroder. So I started writing letters to them. But the plan bombed. I wasn't getting letters back, not even a stamped signature on an 8 by 10. The venture soon became less about competing with my peers and more about my own sense of invisibility and need for validation. I was so desperate to be noticed that I gave up on Hollywood's Brat Pack, as they were known, and started in on those I imagined to be less fatigued by fame: the stars of daytime soap operas.

And *those* people wrote back. Genie Francis from *General Hospital*, Drake Hogestyn from *Days of Our Lives*, Doug Davidson from *The Young and the Restless*. Handwritten notes on postcards! Smiley faces! Autographs!

The niceties were even more notable because what I had written to these actors were inappropriately long letters explaining how I didn't get along with my mother, or about her illness, three or four pages, all of it maudlin. They could have reasonably assumed I was pitching a plotline for an upcoming season of their show. Or maybe their mailboxes were actually full of letters expressing a dissatisfaction like mine, of feeling mismatched and misshapen, at odds with a place, with a body. Maybe these actors had a bin labeled "Misplaced and Transferred Hopes" where they put notes like mine. I'm surprised their gracious replies, their autographs and notes, weren't accompanied by a list of child psychologists in my area. It's true, I wanted help, but being acknowledged sufficed.

A response, *any* response, implied that I existed, that I was not a weirdo, that I'd be okay. I could have gone to a school counselor or even talked to my parents, but I needed someone on TV or in the movies to reach out to me, not because they were famous but because they were so far away, it was like being seen from outer space. Suddenly I didn't feel small; I was bigger than the house I was living in, larger than my town. Thanks to them, I somehow belonged to the world.

I always think about these moments when fans approach me, or write letters, or send messages on social media. I try to recall the sturdiness that comes from recognition.

My other form of validation was through performance. Performing gave me something to do in a given moment in a room. It was a heightened way of relating to people; I could act out feelings instead of dealing with them. Few interactions didn't involve me hamming it up in some way. My sister, Stacey, was my first sidekick, with whom I'd record radio plays or lip-synch for our family using a cane as a microphone. If I was at a friend's house and needed to get home, I insisted on first performing a mock ballet, complete with my friend's ballerina outfit, despite having no dance training whatsoever. Cue "Dance of the Sugar Plum Fairy." That would be followed by a juggling act consisting of two tennis balls and an apple to the tune of the Lovin' Spoonful's "Summer in the City." I loved the ability to be commanding and silly, to focus and control a situation, to elevate the mundane into the theatrical. I wanted people to listen, to witness, or simply to notice me. I held people hostage with this need for attention. It was both an imposition and a plea.

If the following accounts of my attention seeking seem dizzying and unrelenting, that's because they were. I was an anxious child, prone as a baby to colic and frequent tears, and later to fist-pounding, leg-kicking tantrums. My mother likened my melodrama to the silent-film actress Sarah Bernhardt, as if my frustrations and feelings weren't normal but calculated, contrived. Bernhardt's excuse for her theatrics was that she had no sound in her films, whereas mine was an effort to drown out an encroaching family muteness.

At night I'd wake up terrified of fire, death, and disease. The smell of toast, my mother in the kitchen and hungry at three a.m., wafted upstairs. Smoke signals of distress that hung over my sleep. I'd check the pillow to make sure all my hair wasn't falling out. I researched fire escape ladders and calculated the jump from my second-story bedroom window to the nearest tree branch. I'd drag my bedsheets down the hall, sneak into my parents' room, and sleep on the floor. Or I'd crawl into bed with my sister, who would wake up and kick me out. I didn't want to be alone. My brain rarely quieted. In a family video featuring an anniversary message to my grandparents, my voice never falls below the volume of an NFL coach. I won't stop stepping into frame. I didn't want the recording to end.

When I was five or six years old, if my parents had friends over, I would request that I be allowed to sing along to one of my father's records before going to bed. It was a warped suburban version of the children in *The Sound of Music* serenading and charming the adults with "So Long, Farewell" before their bedtime, except that I was singing along to the Eagles, a tune likely about cocaine or driving recklessly in a California highway fast lane. "We stabbed it with our steely knives, but we just couldn't kill the beast," I yelped, off-key. Lullaby, and good night. I bowed, then dragged my baby blanket to my bedroom.

With a recorder on our couch in Bellevue.

I acted as a neighborhood impresario, trying to gather the other children to put on plays or perform hokey talent shows. One summer we formed Lil' "d" Duran Duran, a Duran Duran cover band, except that we only mimed along to the music. We nailed scrap wood together to form guitars and keyboards and painted them with leftover house paint—thus all the instruments were gray—drawing black squiggly strings with Sharpie pens, the keys on the synthesizer uneven rectangles like a bad set of teeth. We practiced every day on my neighbor's deck. (West Coast suburban decks are their own strange art form, elaborate and multilayered, like wooden wedding cakes. Check out old issues of *Sunset* magazine if you want to see how a hot tub might look nestled into a corner or how to plant geraniums between benches for a touch of color. Stain your deck every year.) There was a boom box connected to an extension cord that snaked out from the kitchen, "The Reflex" and "Rio" blasted on repeat with the help of someone hitting the rewind button. Misty and Ricky, an aged German shepherd and an Aussie mix, were our only audience. Our "drummer," Peter, was hard to track down, even though it was his deck on which we were rehearsing. I was both Simon Le Bon, the lead singer—not lip-synching but singing along *over* the music—and our band's promoter. I asked my dad to photocopy flyers for our show at his office. He obliged. But after two weeks of practice everyone but me lost interest. The members of Lil' "d" returned to other summer activities: catching up on soap operas, front-yard water slides fashioned from tarps and a garden hose, tanning while reading V. C. Andrews books, and badminton.

In elementary school, our music teacher occasionally designated a day for sharing. Kids would bring in their parents' ABBA records, or we'd sing along to a Beatles song scrubbed clean of drug references ("We say 'hi!' with a little help from our friends"). One week I decided to perform a dance to the McCoys song "Hang On Sloopy." Children, even less so than adults, often have little concept of genre or even of a song's actual meaning; all songs are kids' songs once they hear them. I liked "Hang On Sloopy" because it sounded like it was a tune about the dog "Snoopy." And so I wanted to do a dance for Snoopy, and thus for everyone else in my fifth-grade music class.

The dance I choreographed—and I use the term "choreography" loosely, the way you'd call adding milk to cereal "cooking"—was a combination of marching and punching, and probably resembled aerobics being done by a penguin. I was not graceful. I was coordinated, athletic, and fit, but very gawky. I wore an oversized raspberry-colored T-shirt, the sleeves too long to be called short and too short to be called long, more like flaps. My gangly arms, spiky-haired on account of a misunderstanding I had had about shaving and what body parts to apply a razor to, poked through the sleeves/tubes/flaps like prickly noodles. I tucked the shirt into cream-colored shorts with an elastic band. If not for a fresh knee scab, one might not have been able to tell where my pale legs began and the shorts ended. I can still recall Mrs. Pappas going up to a boy named Braden—whose mouth was only capable of one expression, a smirk—and saying, "Try not to laugh." But I danced anyway. I hung on, like Sloopy.

In a junior high government class, our teacher held a mock trial. I played the mother of the accused. The roles were set: a defense attorney, a prosecutor, the witnesses for each side, the judge, the jury. It was a routine classroom exercise that would take up a few days of our time and help the students learn about the judicial process. Our teacher handed out sheets of evidence for the lawyers to consult, while the rest of us sat around, bored, waiting to take the stand and answer a few questions before returning to a slouched posture and watching the clock. Deciding that the event needed an infusion of energy, and dissatisfied with the binary and predictable outcome of the trial—guilty or not guilty, how banal!—I decided to stage a confession. I waited for a lull in order to amplify the drama. Then I stood up from my desk and shouted, "My son is innocent. I am the killer!"

All heads turned toward me. There was laughter but I didn't care. My teacher looked dumbfounded as I strolled up to take the stand. This was *my* trial now. I then extemporized a ten-minute confession that explained where I'd hidden the weapon and outlined my revenge-based motive, all told with a shaky voice and a trembling lower lip.

I felt victorious. I had pulled off something both ridiculous and unpredictable. But not everyone was pleased. My classmate Tim, the defense lawyer, took me aside afterward, eyes brimming with tears. He told me that his dad had a brain tumor and on top of that I'd just ruined his chances of winning the case. I felt horrible about his father but vaguely satisfied that I had rescued our class from another mundane afternoon of expected outcomes. As a performer personality seeking attention, this was a frequent intersection of emotions.

In high school I held a series of "How to Host a Murder" parties at my house. In case you are unfamiliar, HTHAM was a series of role-playing mystery games with near-legitimate sounding names like "The Chicago Caper" and "Grapes of Frath." I've played almost all of them. The game requires eight guests—there are four male roles and four female roles—all of whom are assigned characters, each a suspect in a classic tale of mystery and suspense. One of them—gasp!—is the murderer. As a surprise to absolutely no one, not a single male friend of mine ever wanted to participate, so four of my girlfriends always had to come to the party dressed in drag. Also unsurprisingly, I took the game *very* seriously.

I sent out the invitation weeks before. I asked that my friends dress up, and costume suggestions were included in the invite. After all, this wasn't a low-rent, fly-by-night, wear-what-you-want-and-add-a-name-tag situation; no, we had to *embody* our characters. If that meant you

How to Host a Murder party.

had to go to a costume shop to rent a flapper dress or hit up a thrift store for a vintage military uniform, so be it. Bowler hats, swords, briefcases, golf clubs, garter belts, pearls: yes to all of it.

I didn't slack with my hosting duties, either. I got out the special-occasion candle holders and polished the silver, onto which I placed pizza bites, piping hot from the microwave. I rinsed off the crystal champagne flutes—to my knowledge this was the only time they were ever used—and filled them with sparkling cider. For "Powar and Greede," which took place during the Golden Age of Hollywood, I replaced our framed family photos with magazine pictures of movie stars from the era. Good-bye to the Brownsteins posing in front of the fireplace, trying to keep our dog Buffy in frame; hello, Lana Turner! And Elizabeth Taylor and James Stewart looked far more sophisticated than any gap-toothed, mosaic-vest-clad school photo my sister or I had ever taken. I even went so far as to autograph the celebrity photos, making the signatures out to the host of this particular game, the towering head of Powar Studios, W. Anton Powar.

Brownstein family holiday card. Redmond, Washington.

Before the festivities began, I banished my father and sister to the TV room. I pressed play on the mixtape I'd made containing the decade-appropriate music and dimmed the lights. The guests arrived and we mingled in character for a while. We gave toasts, ate sliced cheddar atop buttery crackers, and admired one another's outfits and accoutrements. We slow-danced, girls with mustaches swaying back and forth with girls in dresses. Then we sat down on Ethan Allen upholstered chairs and solved a murder.

I suppose I had reached my limits of mere participation and pretend. I wasn't really creating anything; I was facilitating, implementing, setting up situations that could be both fantastical and fantasy. It was ultimately silly; it was a game. What I loved was the role-playing, the gender ambiguity, the hints of sexiness and bravado, the moments that deviated from the rules and structure. Dressing up and performing allowed me to play at and try on identities, teleporting me into adulthood, into other worlds, into characteristics that would feel foreign in my own skin and my own clothes, but not if I was someone else.

I had yet to find the medium or the vessel through which I could harness my anxiety and restlessness—my yearning to be understood, into something both pointed and vast. That shape needed for my creative hunger would come eventually.

It took a while for me to get there.

But first I should go back and explain how I ended up hanging out with the kind of people who played music.

In elementary school, I was confident and thus well liked, popular even. I was an early-round draft pick for teams in PE class, I won the spelling bee, I attended every crucial water park birthday party and sleepover, I was active in music, sports, and school plays, and I was elected vice president. (My campaign speech included lines like "Girls just wanna have fun, but they want to be politicians, too." And, "We built this city on rock 'n' roll, but we should build this *school* upon leadership." When I finished talking, I played recorded snippets of all the songs I'd mentioned, in case anyone had the nerve or cluelessness to miss my clever puns and pop culture references.)

By sixth grade I had two best friends, one of whom, Tammy, was the first person I knew whose parents were divorced. She lived with her mom. Tammy was also the first kid I knew who lived in an apartment. At that age I thought apartments were built specifically to house the single or the newly single, a divorce dormitory of sorts. Tammy was cute and tough, with freckles and an upturned ski-jump nose, her bangs bleached tangerine from hydrogen peroxide and sprayed into an upright, frozen wave. Her mom was a smoker, also a rarity to me in the Pacific Northwest suburbs, but I liked the lived-in quality the smell of nicotine brought to their place, a gritty, world-weary sophistication. Plus, we stole her mom's cigarettes so that we could smoke in parks and on weekends. Smoking for me meant blowing outward like you would on a kazoo. In my mind it still looked cool, and I was too afraid to inhale. I credit this early exposure to cigarettes with removing any desire to be a smoker later in life. (Parents, take note.)

When Tammy arrived at Benjamin Rush Elementary, the rumor was that she had already lost her virginity. She tacitly and vaguely confirmed this to be true, though I still think the whole story might have been fabricated. I figured it might be a case of crafty social maneuvering on her part, a self-mythologizing that is granted to—or required by—kids who transfer schools. Or maybe Tammy was trying to suggest that she had some form of street cred, which is one way a kid with lower economic status gets on equal footing with the middle-class kids. Anything that smelled of real-life experience or hardship (the more exotic and subversive, the better) the comfortable suburban kids held in high esteem. This notion of personal transformation and redefinition is what drew me to Tammy: there was a boldness, a mystery, and a whole lot of not giving a shit.

It was Tammy who orchestrated my first kisses and make-outs. Together we attended summer camp: me, so I could shoot bows and arrows, sing Harry Chapin's "Cat's in the Cradle" in a round, and make lanyards; her, so she could meet boys from other schools and gargle with someone else's tongue. Eventually, I decided that holding hands with a guy in a turtleneck and shorts in the middle of the woods and dancing to Depeche Mode in the mess hall was more fun than canoeing or collecting clams on the beach, though it was always in the back of my mind that I hadn't showered or been able to go to the bathroom for over five days.

After camp, on a springtime backyard tent sleepover, Tammy arranged for a group of boys to sneak in. She instructed each of us, paired us up, and told us how to use our tongues when we kissed, which as a preteen is an unrelenting technique that requires one's mouth to be open longer and wider than during a dental exam. Tammy zipped herself into a sleeping bag with a boy. The rest of us were sitting upright, not sure what to do horizontally and thus not wanting to commit to one person. We traded kisses in a humid tent that smelled of Drakkar Noir, cigarettes, and mint liqueur. Almost immediately I cut the lips of a kid named Ricky with my braces. I retired for the night; I felt inept at this carefree, outdoorsy, group sexiness, but I made an eager, loyal follower. I liked being part of a gang.

Jennifer was my other friend. She had an older brother named Michael whose heavy-metal tape collection I admired: Iron Maiden, Judas Priest, Van Halen. More important, however, her aunt worked for Huey Lewis. Jennifer had a framed picture of him in the house. That fact alone was enough for her family to seem magical to me. My connection to this rock star with countless hits on the radio and whose albums I owned was clearly tenuous—it was my friend's aunt, whom I'd never met and who didn't live in Redmond and who possibly was no longer working for Huey Lewis or for the News. Maybe she had done a job for him at some point? Or she had talked about working for him? Maybe she had wanted to? Maybe she was employed by someone, but not by Huey Lewis? Maybe, like me, she was a fan of his album *Sports*. The facts were mutable and hard to pin down, but there *was* that framed photo. And that was something, something real. And I had been in the house with that photo. And that person in the photo was famous. These are the ways fans maneuver through the world, with flimsy connections and strong hopes.

Despite all the sleepovers, or the sneaking out to drape toilet paper over someone's house, or the weeks at summer camp together, Tammy, Jennifer, and I drifted apart once we entered junior high. But they were my cohorts during my happiest childhood years, the ones during which my mom was healthy and present enough to help me with my homework, not to mention that ridiculous election speech, and when it didn't seem odd that my dad bought a motorcycle and drove off to Canyonlands on a vacation with a male buddy.

CHAPTER 3

DISAPPEARANCE

I first heard the term "anorexic" in the backseat of a car on the way home from the movies. It was the summer before seventh grade. From the burgundy insides of a Chevy Blazer, we all turned to look at a jogger, a woman, a sinewy form devoid of curves, angles only, rib cage and clavicles protruding, like some sort of moving body diagram, inside out. The driver of the car, my friend's mother, said the word that we did not know. What it described was what we had just seen: a skeleton in Nikes.

The word "anorexia" was like a prize I had won in a drawing someone entered for me on my behalf; unexpected, sure, but I would find a use for it. And I did. At the dinner table I inserted it into the conversation. I added it to the lyrics of popular songs and sang them while my mother slowly pushed her food around a plate, rarely lifting the fork to her mouth, every morsel a lame horse on a track, never reaching the finish line. I taunted my mother with the word as if anorexia were something she might desire, not something she already had.

My mother was fair-skinned with a delicate, bony strand of a nose and dark, straight hair. Her eyes were a deep brown, and I think of her as unblinking, as if she were always looking at something suspended between horror and sadness. She smiled with a strained, hesitant warmth. In the years before my mother's illness, it's not her body that I recall being different, though obviously it *was*—her cheeks fuller and brighter, her hair shinier, her breasts and stomach softer—but rather her presence. She was noticeable: she was in the car and in the kitchen, putting curlers in her hair and shopping for clothes, talking with her friends, helping me with my homework, attending school plays, walking, talking, sitting, eating, being, existing.

In a photo from several years later, the last family vacation we would ever take, my mother is standing on the beach in Hawaii. Bikini-clad, burnt red like she'd been dipped in cherry Kool-Aid, bags of white pus forming on her sternum, bones for days. Thin, brittle hair—it had been falling out for a while now. Hollow eyes and cheeks. She is somewhere between rotting and a fossil. Maybe she hoped that the smaller she got, the easier it would be to disappear.

After consulting a doctor and nutritionist, and probably not at all on account of my singing or tormenting, my mother finally did admit—to us, to her friends, to herself—that she was ill. And when I was fourteen, she checked herself into an eating disorder unit at a hospital in Ballard. She would be gone nearly a month.

For the first two weeks my mom was away our kitchen was stocked with covered dishes prepared for my father, sister, and me by various women at my dad's law firm. Casseroles mostly. Heat and serve. If you saw our crowded fridge, it might look like we were preparing for a big party, like the Super Bowl, or an unnamed celebration wherein the family stuff themselves while their wife or mother is in the hospital on account of starving herself. There was a dish consisting of tortilla chips, cheese, chicken, and a cream-of-something cream-colored, the final ingredient being the only one distinguishing it from nachos. This became our instant favorite. My dad learned how to make the tortilla casserole, we alternated those nights with bagel dogs, soft pretzels, or tamales from Costco, and we soon realized we might be able to survive on our own. In hindsight, I'm glad we had this time to practice.

Meanwhile, at junior high school and among my peers, I was mildly enjoying the attention that having a mother in the hospital granted me. An illness in the family felt like the currency I needed to make myself more interesting. In home economics class we watched health movies that addressed the concerns of body dysmorphia, a TV special called *Little Miss Perfect*, and one about bulimia, *Kate's Secret*, starring Meredith Baxter Birney. I felt as knowledgeable as the teacher and acted accordingly. I broke down the difference between bingeing and purging. I explained what ipecac was. And, yes, I said, with a hint of disbelief, bulimics sometimes hide bags of vomit under their beds. My mom was 88 pounds and anorexic, but apparently I had the market cornered on all eating disorders. I wasn't the prettiest or the smartest one in school, I was desperate for a clear role among my friends, and now I had one. I was someone they felt sorry for.

I also had a newfound status on the carpool circuit. I rode shotgun everywhere. While my friends were in the backseat discussing bra sizes and boys, I sat in the front and listened while their mothers opened up about a recent MS diagnosis, spousal drinking, and kitchen remodels. Trash compactors! Skylights! My own mother's condition was a floodgate; apparently now I could understand something that these women's daughters could not. We traded diseases and misfortunes, swapped them like baseball cards. I stared at the car radio knobs or the fading "5" of the gear shift, empathically nodding my head with the certainty of a scrubs-wearing career nurse on a lunch break. "It will be a long struggle, yes." "You'll get through it."

As my friends embarked on adolescence, developing what seemed to be a natural, God-given talent for makeup and hair removal, my nose grew too big, my gums appeared to be sliding down my two front teeth, and my chest and back remained indistinguishable from each other. I felt the confidence of my younger self slipping away. But that didn't matter to their moms. And I imagine it was they who kept me on invite lists to birthday parties, weekend ski trips, and after-school mall excursions. After all, who else among their kids' friends was mature enough to understand the nuanced joys of a recently procured coffee-table book on the Kennedys or the acquisition of a delicious chocolate fondue recipe? Plus, I was their number-one source for scene-by-scene summaries of films they were too harried to see. I stood next to them in the kitchen while they unloaded the dishwasher, sipping lemonade, casually leaning against the counter or sitting atop it, retelling the plots of *Clue* and *Romancing the Stone* from title sequence to end credits. Meanwhile, my friend worked on homework or chatted on the phone in the other room. That was child's play. I felt adult, important.

When a friend's father died of Lou Gehrig's disease, her mother counted me among the first to be notified. I was getting ready for school when I received the call; I took the news like a pro. No tears. When was the funeral? Did they need anything? Later, in the school bathroom during lunch, I delivered the story to our other friends with the gravity and stoicism of a nightly-news anchor. Here were the facts. They wept streams of turquoise mascara while I stood near the paper towel dispenser and let them know that this was just how things were. This was life. Tough it out.

But the reality of my mom being in the eating disorders unit was far less glamorous and a lot more painful. There was little to brag about.

Kenny and Linda. My parents before they were married. Chicago, Illinois.

My parents grew up in the Chicago area, my father in Evanston, my mother in Skokie. They met at the University of Illinois at Urbana-Champaign when my dad was in law school and my mom was an undergrad. For their wedding anniversary they drove a VW bus to Seattle, the city where I would be born. I know very little about my parents' childhoods; the historical facts are hazy and scattered. My father's dad was a doctor, his mother a housewife; "Dr. and Mrs. Stanley Brownstein" said the return address on the birthday and Valentine's Day cards we received from them, containing either a five-dollar bill or a five-dollar check. My mother's parents were less well-off. Her father was an accountant, then a comptroller in the auto industry. Her mother was a teacher.

Before my father sold my childhood home in Redmond to move to Seattle, I dug through boxes in the garage, salvaging old books and photos.

I found letters my father and mother had written back and forth when they were engaged. He was working for the Washington state D.A. and she was still in college. My mother's notes were sweet and longing; she expressed a yearning to be reunited, to be out of Illinois, to start a life. My father wrote considerate but formal responses, largely about his job and the Pacific Northwest.

At holidays, descriptions of relatives were not about how they lived but rather how they died. My paternal grandmother would point to the faces in pictures and rattle off every kind of cancer you could think of—and ones you couldn't think of. I'd tune into stories about our family, hoping to glean insight, only to have them quickly be disputed and left unfinished. Someone might mention an older brother or a baby, a vacation they once embarked on, a profession or a hobby, but the conversation inevitably and quickly devolved into a debate about the meaning of second cousins versus first cousins once removed. We never settled that debate, nor did I ever learn any solid information about my relatives or my family's past.

These convivial but otherwise circuitous talks are likely why my dad's brother, Uncle Mike, often stepped up as the family storyteller and entertainer. When I was younger, my uncle was a thrice-married plastic surgeon (he's now with his fourth wife, my aunt Denise) who had become one of the first and foremost sexual reassignment surgeons in America, specializing in top surgery for female-to-male transgender people. He was also—and still is—a life member of the NRA as well as a benefactor member, and he has voted conservative in every major election. He was passionate about all of it despite how strange this combination of traits might have appeared to others. A typical Thanksgiving involved him describing how a clitoris could be elongated into a penis or trying to explain the notion of "transgender" to a great-aunt who resembled a drag queen, her bony fingers drenched in costume jewelry clicking like a tap shoe routine as she gestured, hands flying up in the air to emphasize her bewilderment. One Thanksgiving my sister and cousin and I played catch with a silicone breast implant my uncle had lying around, while the movie *Scarface* played on the TV in the background. Another Thanksgiving, my grandmother sat at the dining table with taut skin and visible staples in her head from a recent facelift courtesy of one son, while the other son carved into the turkey with an electric knife.

Our family liked to focus on activities instead of communication, so when we weren't tossing around fake breasts or staging photos of relatives snorting flour off the counter to look like cocaine, we got the guns out. When my grandfather retired from medicine, he and my grandmother moved to Tucson, Arizona, which is where he developed an interest

*My sister Stacey pointing a real gun at me in the backyard of
our grandparents' home in Tucson, Arizona.*

in collecting firearms and going to the shooting range. The grandkids loved to pose for pictures on the backyard brick patio, the bright orange Tucson sun and cactus-covered landscape behind us, our unloaded weapons pointed at the camera or, more likely, right at each other.

Though my family didn't talk much to one another, we did talk *about* one another. My dad's parents would refer to their daughter-in-law as "her" or "she," talking as if my mother were invisible even though she sat right there at the table. "Does she ever eat?" they would say to my father. "Does she know how skinny she looks?" I suppose we were better observers than communicators; we were all subjects to be worried over, complained about, even adored, but never quite people to be held or loved. There was an intellectual, almost absurd distance.

The ways that oddity and detachment intersected in the family might best be summed up in the story of the family dog. Buffy, a forty-pound golden retriever mix we adopted from the pound when I was six and my sister was three, had been smothered with love in her youth. Buffy, for whom we took a pet first-aid class in order to learn how to be responsible owners, who was the muse for my grade-school poetry exercises ("Buffy is fluffy!"), our sidekick for picnics and outings, on the sidelines for soccer games, and the subject most featured in my first roll of film— posing on my baby blanket and wearing sunglasses—after I was given a camera for my birthday. Buffy, who followed us around the cul-de-sacs while we engaged in dirt clod fights with the neighbor kids, and trotted after us while we rode Big Wheels and eventually bikes. Buffy, who suffered the sting of the archaic idea that you could punish a dog by smacking it on the nose with a rolled-up newspaper and whose tail was run over by my mother as she backed the car out of the driveway. And Buffy, turned back into a stray in her own home on account of the rest of us surrendering to emptiness, drifting away from anything we could call familiar, her skin itching and inflamed, covered with sores and bites, like tattoos, like skywriting, screaming with redness due to an allergy, as if to say *Please, please pet me!* But we didn't. When we had to put her down, not because she was sick but because she was old and neglected— a remnant of a family we no longer recognized—my father asked my sister to do it. My sister was sixteen. She drove the dog to the vet one day after school by herself. No one else said good-bye.

After I was given my first camera I set up many photo shoots. Here I am posing atop my baby blanket with an asymmetrical haircut, my Cabbage Patch Kid, a Snugglebum toy, and my dog Buffy.

The distance and detachment created a loneliness. We couldn't name the source of it, but there was a blankness around which we gathered, one that grew colder and darker, and seeped into everything we did. I think for my mother it was most pronounced. I would lie in bed at night and hear her on the phone with my father, who was away for weeks on business in Europe or Asia or Australia. She was crying, scared, frustrated, lonely. Her anxiety made her brittle, easy to anger. But I didn't feel sympathetic. I felt fear, neglect. I felt resentment.

My mother and I started to fight all the time. She was retreating from the world, a slow-motion magic trick. Meanwhile, I was getting louder, angrier, wilder. I experimented with early forms of my own amplification—of self, of voice, of fury—while my mother's volume was turned down lower and lower, only ever audible when she broadcast searing feedback and static; broken, tuneless sounds. We vacillated between shouting and silence, the megaphone and the mute. We scrapped and scraped. I'd rile her up until medicine bottles were hurled my way and I responded with a piece of pizza. She threatened to wear a raincoat in the house so she could deal with "all of the flying shit." Everything was a projectile, an indoor hailstorm.

The first time we visited my mother in the eating disorder unit of the hospital, the thing she thought to warn us about was not her own condition but that some of the other patients shopped at thrift stores and that we shouldn't judge. Her upwardly mobile sense of middle-class decorum was still intact, despite the fact that *her* clothing drooped, almost slithered, off her body as if it were seeking elsewhere to perch, looking hardly different on her than it would on a wire hanger.

In her concern and preoccupation over how we might handle the class and lifestyle differences in the EDU, she neglected to mention that her roommate in the hospital was my exact age. Breanna was a goth, a cool city kid with black hair, blunt bangs, and a knack for liquid eyeliner. She might have been the exact kind of girl I'd be friends with, or who I'd want to actually *be*, but right now she was my mom's friend and confidante. While I had discussed my mom's illness with my friends' parents, I had never thought to talk about it with my own mother. And now there was a surrogate me. Breanna could share and understand the one thing about my mother that I never could, her disease. Later, after they were both released, they'd hang out and watch movies together, grown-up movies, like the film adaptation of Marilynne Robinson's *Housekeeping*, that I had no interest in. I felt sophomoric and callow, but I was only fourteen. Plus, I didn't want a friend, I wanted a mom.

Like any part of a hospital, an eating disorder unit has a smell. The smell is like a color that doesn't have a recognizable hue, an Easter egg dipped into every kind of dye until it possesses an unnamed ugliness. It is beige, it is skin, it is bile. The EDU smelled like protein-rich powder supplements and chemical cleaners, like a hot, stinging exhale of despair.

Visiting hours consisted of filling in my mom about our lives, attending group therapy, taking walks through the hallways, and participating in activities like ceramics, where we'd glaze clay dinosaurs and mugs to take home with us later. Souvenirs. It was hard not to stare at the shapes that surrounded us: a girl whose body was so emaciated that she was covered in a layer of fine hair, walking near another woman whose skin had stretched and stretched to contain some bottomless need, a self-hugging device, a house. The bulimics scared me the least so I focused my attention on them; they looked relatively healthy on the outside, as long as you didn't look too closely at their vomit-stained teeth.

Puberty was a confusing time to be around so many women whose bodies had become a sort of battleground. My own relationship to food was healthy. I was lean and athletic with a high metabolism. I could eat half a pizza with a side of breadsticks and wash it down with soda. I never dieted or denied myself food. But there were ways in which I started to disconnect from my body during this time; that's where the sadness was, not just mine but these other women's as well. I lodged myself firmly in my head. It was the only way to process all that I witnessed at the EDU, those halls of hungry ghosts.

In my vast experience of visiting hospitals, I've noticed that part of the job of being a visitor is to make a show of looking healthy and able: running around, skipping, laughing *really* loud, having a big appetite, illustrating athletic prowess. Otherwise it's as if a doctor or nurse or psychiatrist might look at you and decide that you have to check in and stay. Or that the vulnerability, heartache, and fear will leave you open to illness—you'll enter healthy and leave enervated, or not leave at all. A visitor can't show weakness. Thus, my sister and I played very competitive Ping-Pong in the common room for everyone to see, and to hear. LOOK. AT. US. NOTHING. WRONG. AT ALL. It was almost like we had dropped in to play a pickup game, and there just happened to be a bunch of sick people in the hospital.

On the day my mother left we participated in a "coining ceremony," wherein she said good-bye to her fellow eating disorder friends and hello to her family, to us. The coining ceremony was similar to the "share circles" of group therapy, except that it was solely focused on the patient who was getting out. Everyone read something from their journal about my mother. As I listened I sensed that within this configuration of fellow patients my mother was a known entity, she felt cared for and safe, seen. But I was outside the circle. My mother was a stranger to me. My sister was eager to be a part of whatever form my mother was taking on; she melted, molded herself to the dynamic. I didn't want to engage with the illness; the anorexia was what was taking my mother away. I was surprised to find that I was such a focus of the narrative in the room, my mother's desire to be closer to me, my feistiness and anger and alienation a piece of some puzzle I couldn't see the edges of.

Everyone was sobbing, including my father. It was the first time I'd seen him cry. It was like an irrigation system, each person a sprinkler, all watering the room with their tears. I felt drenched, soggy. I wanted everyone to be stronger, to embrace the stoicism I was perfecting. I judged. These weak women and their diseases. Eat already, or stop eating. Get it together! The fragility was suffocating, the dysmorphia so pronounced it made my head hurt. The two-dimensional anorexics and the three-dimensional claymation overeaters—no matter the size of their own sense of insubstantiality, each had taken on the form of her disease. It made me hungry and empty, too, but not for food. I was hungry for family, for strength, for wholeness.

On the day my mom was released from the hospital, we stopped at a grocery store on the way home. A horrible idea on my father's part, or maybe it was my mom's idea, to show off the cure, a victory lap through the cookie aisle, an acceptance speech in front of the pasta. I don't know if you'd take an alcoholic to a liquor store on the way home from rehab but maybe it's different with food. The idea was to normalize it, so we tried. I spent the entire grocery store trip telling my mom about the TV shows she had missed while she was in the hospital. This was to distract her from the fact that we were surrounded by everything she didn't want to eat. I'd feed her with stories! I'd entertain the pain right out of her.

When we got back to the house there was a sign above the garage door, "Welcome Home." I'm certain that when my mother saw it she wanted to turn right around and go back to the EDU. Who wants to advertise that they are home from the hospital, unless they're bringing home a baby? It was glaring blitheness on my father's part. Maybe my mom *was* a newborn, coming home to be loved and nurtured in all the ways that could keep her healthy and in recovery. It was a do-over. The welcome turned out to be temporary anyhow. Within a year she left for good.

CHAPTER 4

NO NORMAL

One of my earliest childhood memories is my father taking me in the evening to Samena Swim & Recreation Club in Bellevue. It was just him and me. I'd taken swim lessons and could hang out by myself with the help of water wings, goggles, and a kickboard while my father swam laps in a nearby lane. I loved the echo in the cavernous room, the way the sounds and voices melded into each other, gurgling, muted, watercolors for the ears. I spun around, did the dead man's float, watched pale, distorted legs dangle down into the blue. I kept one eye on my dad and another on the pool's edge, my two sources of safety.

Too young to get changed in the women's locker room alone, I'd accompany my father to the men's area. Once my clothes were tugged back over my arms and legs, sticky from inadequate toweling off, dampness seeping through in the creases but warm nonetheless, I'd wait for my father to shower and dress. As I sat there I wasn't looking anywhere in particular: at the rubber mats on the floor, the slats in the bench, at pale toes like gnarled gingerroots, calves with hair worn off in patches from dress socks, and knees everywhere, those scrunched-up, featureless faces. "Stop staring," my dad would insist over and over again, sounding admonishing and embarrassed. I kept my head down. Later I realized that this reminder, this reprimand, was likely something my father was saying to himself more than to me. The shame of looking, of wanting to look.

And then there was that time we were pulling the car into the garage and from the backseat I yelled the word "penis" for no reason other than that I was eight years old and at that age it's fun to call out the words for genitalia in a loud voice. One day I'd come home from kindergarten and repeated a term I'd heard on the playground: "mother fucker two-ball bitch." Whether it was at my ignorant daring or at the perplexity of the phrase itself, I'm not sure, but my parents laughed. Here I was now going for the encore. But saying "penis" in front of my father, while he was trapped in a car with me, and thus trapped with that word, and whatever he pictured in his mind when he heard that word, whatever feelings he felt about that word, that thing, resulted in me being dragged upstairs and getting my mouth washed out with soap.

Oh, we also received the International Male catalog, a men's underwear catalog that is essentially a showcase for big European cocks.

Only in retrospect can I find clues to my father's gayness. Sometimes the dull detritus of our pasts become glaring strands once you realize they form a pattern, a lighted path to the present. I have to turn over and reimagine certain moments from my childhood and make them conform to a different narrative, a different outcome.

When my sister and I were both away at college, my father, still living in the house we grew up in, informed us that he was going to start taking in "boarders." I imagined something out of a W. Somerset Maugham novel: doilies, stale biscuits, afternoon tea, a collision of international seekers. Except our house was in the suburbs, carpeted, with an open layout, replete with landings and those bulked-up banisters that were good for jumping off when adults weren't around, or for hide-and-seek stealthiness. The playroom, with its sloped ceiling, old striped couch, and first-generation CD player, would be the "room for rent." The idea of a boarder seemed odd, even seedy. I was indignant. This was a childhood home, not a hostel!

It wasn't for financial reasons. My father's rationale was that the house was unnecessarily big for one person—true. And empty—also true. I suppose he was staving off loneliness. They were always men or college-aged boys. They were unlike my father: One was a snowboarder with beachy, blond hair whose family owned a water sports business. Another was a part-time musician who sold me an Ampeg amplifier head and cabinet that he was storing in the garage. *My* garage! One man I know nothing about save for the fact that his car was repossessed right there in the driveway. If they had one thing in common it was that all of them were slightly wayward, rough-hewn, jocose. I would occasionally come home on the weekends and no longer feel like the house was a retreat, or even mine—I was simply crashing there like anyone else. There was a new sense of transience to the house, of transition. It was a husk, emptied of sentimentality, populated by strangers, and by that I don't just mean these men, I also mean my father. I am certain nothing happened between the renters and my dad. The men, the boys, were unaware, in between and on their way. But for my father this was a rehearsal, a way of circling around a new kind of male intimacy.

My father was a corporate lawyer. He went to work in a suit and tie. He had a secretary. He left the house before seven a.m. His professional life felt generic, like a backdrop, a signifier more than a life: OFFICE JOB. I knew very little about what he did. He traveled to China, Russia, Australia, sending home postcards and returning with stuffed koala bears or wooden nesting dolls. He collected toy trucks and paraphernalia with company insignia that he displayed atop credenzas or that my sister and I would grudgingly mix in with our other toys, as if we didn't want to sully our Cabbage Patch dolls or My Little Ponies with crass corporate sponsorship. My dad had work friends whom we saw infrequently. It was all trousers and ties. Grays and browns. There was a sterility to it that I found both exotic and comforting. The office was in a 1970s high-rise next to a mall. A swift-moving elevator, a destination we'd reach undeterred, a telephone number I had memorized, a secretary who knew my name.

My father wasn't just taciturn—it was like he didn't want to be heard.

With my sister Stacey, holding stuffed koalas that our father
brought back from a business trip to Australia.

I don't know if he had nothing to say or if he didn't know what to say. Perhaps his reticence came from not being able to name what or who he was, or what he felt. So he stayed quiet, and he waited for the words to find him.

This is what I knew about my father: He grew up in Evanston, Illinois, outside of Chicago. He attended Duke University and then the University of Illinois at Urbana-Champaign for law school. He has one brother. He was the assistant coach of my soccer team, and the head coach of my sister's. He ran marathons. He mowed the lawn. He was always working on something called a sump pump in the crawl space. He was slight and handsome, dark-eyed, wide-eyed, wide-nostrilled, looking curious and confounded, boyish. He was stern yet timid, a disciplinarian with no follow-through, self-conscious, not prone to affection, undemonstrative. He liked liver pâté. He had a mustache and then he didn't; I cried when he shaved it off because I didn't know he had a space between the bottom of his nose and his upper lip, like a pale secret.

My father was hard to know, and gave little indication that there was much to know. He claimed he remembered almost nothing about his childhood. He only ever recalled one incident. It was about the first time he came home from college on holiday break. He was sitting in his parents' home, waiting for my grandfather to return from work. When my grandfather came through the door, he greeted the family dog first, even though he and the hound had only been apart for the day and my father had been gone for months. That's the story.

My father came out to me in the summer of 1998. I was headed to Seattle from Olympia to pick up a friend at the airport. She wasn't arriving until almost midnight, so the plan was to stop in on my father and then visit some friends after their soundcheck at the Crocodile Café.

My father was at his first apartment in Seattle. He had sold the Red-mond house, a nontraumatic event, probably for the best considering it had become a house for wayward youth. I was relieved he was out of the suburbs, especially Redmond, changed so fiercely by Microsoft, trans-formed into a corporate headquarters, indistinguishable from the brand. It was as though you could see an architect's model as you walked around; it had an exemplary quality, both a place and a placeholder.

Seattle felt like a good spot for my father. Though he'd been living there for a while now, his apartment had that strange first-apartment feel, always odd for someone you associate with the accumulation of things. Parents are supposed to be our storage facilities: insert a mem-ory, let them hold on to it for you. Leave behind stuffed animals and school projects, report cards and clothes, they keep them so you don't have to. I knew that wasn't part of the bargain with my family. I've thrown out piles of things, taken them to the dump and never looked back. But still, to see my dad in a blank space, it only seemed to make him more blurry, like he had just appeared on a canvas, before the back-ground was filled in. His sphere was borderless, and the sense of nowhere made me feel alone, unbound. I'd often felt that around my relatives, but now I felt it anew and acutely. Like the first time my dad bought Christ-mas ornaments and I realized that after wanting to celebrate Christmas for so long, it wasn't about having a tree, it was about having a box in the basement or attic or garage, something that we could return to over and over again, something that said, this is us and this is where we were last year, and this is where we'll stay, and this is where we'll pile on memories, over and over again, until there are so many memories that it's blinding, the brightness of family, the way love and nurturing is like a color you can't name because it's so new. And then my father went out and bought cheap ornaments and we took them out of boxes and plastic and I realized it wasn't Christmas that I wanted. What I wanted was a family.

So here was my father, in this white apartment with textured walls and thick carpeting, and the scant amount of furniture and paintings he'd brought from Redmond, looking like interlopers, like imposters, neither here nor there. And we're sitting in this living room and I have no idea who he is and he says, "So I guess I'm coming out to you." He said it like that, in a sort of meta way, as if he were along for a ride that his new self was taking him on. Which was typical, like he was just a sidekick in his own life, a shadow, though I'm assuming it was more of a linguistic fumbling, not knowing exactly how to come out or what words to use.

I was used to this sort of presentational mode at this point. What I heard was "Your mother is going into the hospital," or "Your mother is moving out," or "I have cancer," and then again a few years later, "I have cancer." I was used to being sat down and presented with life-altering information and taking it with expected nonchalance. This was me asking my friends' parents about MS all over again. My role was to be factual and professional, like a reporter. Emotions were not part of the equation. So, tell me, Dad, how did you know?

What my father explained next was basically the history of the Internet, at least in terms of how we use it for social media and networking. In fact, if it weren't for the Internet, I don't know if my father would have realized, or been able to acknowledge, that he was gay. I thought of Microsoft taking over Redmond, and now gayness taking over my father.

He began in chat rooms. International ones. Asking questions. Talking with other men, many of them married, he made sure to point out. Eventually, it was U.S. chat rooms, exchanging stories, feelings, desires,

telling of trysts and transgressions, confusion, shame, lust. Eventually
he was chatting with other men in Seattle. The truth was a satellite, the
picture getting clearer, circling and homing in, and then he was close
enough to touch it. He met a male nurse named Russ, a friend, someone
he could confide in. And there was a Northwest men's running group.
He was allowing the truth to get closer: it was the galaxy at first, then
global, then the continent, then local, and finally the shape of him, set-
tling in. I don't know what that must have felt like, to realize you have a
body at the age of fifty-five.

The year before, my father had been diagnosed with cancer for the
second time. Kidney. I remembered that right before his surgery he had
taken a business trip to Texas. It seemed strange that his company
wouldn't send someone else, that he would insist on traveling so close to
the surgery. I passed it off as stoicism, not wanting cancer to interrupt
his life or schedule, or just denial. But that night in Seattle he told me
that on an earlier trip he had met a couple in Houston, both lawyers,
gay. The trip he took right before his surgery was to come out to them.
In case he didn't make it. To strangers. In Texas. He put down a small
"x" on a map, a little scrawl of visibility. Then he came home, the doctors
removed the cancer, and he had to live. More important, he wanted to.

I took the news better than my sister. She felt abandoned a second
time: first my mother, and now this. But I, too, felt confused. If he
wasn't himself during my childhood, then what was my childhood?
What was I? When someone says, "That wasn't me, *this* is me," then I
wonder how was I myself around a you who wasn't? My father had been
the constant, the territory, and now I felt like he was rescinding. There
was no longer a placeholder. I would have to discover him anew.

We want our parents to be the norm from which we deviate. So when
my dad came out, my instinct was that I needed to husband-up and get

married. As if my family wasn't freaky enough. Me: adrift. My sister: unmarried. My mom: ? And now my dad. Who would fly the flag of normality? My sister bore this burden more heavily than I did. But I immediately felt like I should be popping out kids within a few years of my dad realizing he was gay. Let our parents be anorexic and gay! That shit is for teenagers. My sister and I would be the adults. We would be conventional, conservative even. Guns, God, country, and my contrarian, reactionary self. (This phase lasted about ten minutes.)

When my father came out to his mom, my grandmother said, "You waited for your father to die, why couldn't you have waited for me to die?" I knew then that I never want to contribute to the corrosiveness of wanting someone to stay hidden. Despite all my initial conflicts about trying to reconcile the father I had as a child to the one I have now, I am thankful that he is happy, that he did not waste another second. Now there is someone to know.

CHAPTER 5

BORN NAKED

In my junior year of high school I formed a band with a few girls called Born Naked. We agonized over band names (though clearly not for long enough) until our singer, Alexis, showed up with a naked picture of her mother when she was pregnant, and that was that. We made stickers, which felt more important than the music itself, and practiced at our drummer Rachel's house. Our amps were the size of shoeboxes. Most of our guy friends were in bands. We didn't take ourselves too seriously, almost as a means of warding off any potential criticism—if we thought of Born Naked as a joke, then no one could make fun of us, we were in on it, we got it. Our signature song was one I'd penned called "You Annoy Me."

Sometimes I think I have barely moved on from that sentiment. So much of my intention with songs is to voice a continual dissatisfaction, or at least to claw my way out of it. The lyrics:

> The way you look really annoys me
> The way you talk really bores me
> You think that you are always right

You keep me awake at night

You're the most annoying person I know

Get out of my life, just go, go, go

We don't care what you say

We're not listening anyway

Don't bother me, don't talk to me

Don't talk talk talk talk to me

The few chords I had learned were courtesy of a neighbor and school friend of mine, Jeremy Enigk, who later became known as the singer and guitarist of the band Sunny Day Real Estate. If I sneaked through a nearby yard, walked up the hill, and down the other side, I could get to Jeremy's adjoining neighborhood, monikers like Ridgemont East segueing into Hampton Place, indistinct except for the name and the smooth newness of the sidewalks. I carried my guitar without a case, out in the open, both shield and sword.

Jeremy was, to quote from a Bikini Kill song, the "star-bellied boy" of my high school. With an angelic voice, bright eyes pooling with color and sadness, and a preternatural gift for melody, he was our genius. We gathered around him on the bus, at lunchtime, and at parties like he was a messiah. He was floppy-haired, cute, and mysterious, shy and funny. But mostly his appeal was that he could sing. He could take all the records we were listening to (Sinéad O'Connor, U2, R.E.M.), deliver an up-close version, and bring them into our world. Jeremy became our conduit, taking these formidable albums and making them feel like ours, as if he were a live Walkman we toted around with us, pressing play whenever we wanted to be reminded of our little friend group, how with enough music, with our eyes closed, we could feel like everything and nothing all at once.

In Jeremy's bedroom he'd show me chords by way of playing "The Last Day of Our Acquaintance" by Sinéad O'Connor. I'd play along to the two-chord song while Jeremy sang. Then he'd get bored and start into R.E.M.'s "The One I Love" or U2's "New Year's Day," both of which required some arpeggiation, and I'd fumble my way through them, often still on the intro as he played the last note. He was patient with me, encouraging. I'd go home and practice, feeling that even with just a few chords, everything was now in my grasp.

At that time, I frequented two record stores: Cellophane Square in the Bellevue Square Mall and Rubato Records, a place owned by an older couple who had played in an early '80s Seattle band called Student Nurse. Rubato was on the first floor of a concrete, two-story office complex in Bellevue. It was there that the clerk recommended I buy two records from a band called Television, not just *Marquee Moon* but *Adventure* as well. He asked if I liked Nirvana, to which I answered yes, and he put in my hands the Shocking Blue LP, which featured the original and much more psychedelic version of "Love Buzz," a song Nirvana covered on *Bleach*. If it weren't for Rubato, I wouldn't own Isaac Hayes records or anything by the Damned. The owners were excited to have an eager and willing explorer, someone whose taste they could influence. Cellophane Square was the more traditional of the two places, with posters on the wall available for purchase that could help demonstrate your music knowledge. Twenty years too late you could display your love for the Clash or Ramones (and I did!), or you could buy a completely unsanctioned Fugazi poster. You could also buy numerous pins or stickers and outfit your jacket or car or notebook with all the outward displays of identity. I drove around the suburbs with a Misfits sticker on my 1979 Honda CVCC, one that referenced their song "Bullet" about the JFK assassination. The sticker depicted an image of Kennedy getting shot in Dallas, blood pouring from his head—a totally offensive and disrespectful image that I nonetheless hoped would let people know that I considered myself a rebel. These things seemed very important. How else could we identify another weirdo or outlier? These symbols intimated a belief system, a way of thinking not just about music but about school and friends and politics and society. It was also a way to separate yourself, to feel bold or try on boldness without yet possessing it. A little inkling of the nonconformist person you could be—you wanted to be—but weren't quite ready to commit to. I papered my walls with band posters and what little I could find in mainstream magazines about alternative and punk, maybe a picture of Babes in Toyland from *Spin* or Fugazi from *Option*. The iconoclast images and iconography covered my room, a jarring contrast to the preppy blue-and-white-striped wallpaper I'd insisted on in elementary school. I resented the parts of myself that were late to adopt coolness, late to learn—I wanted to have always possessed a savviness and sophistication, even though I clearly had neither.

Born Naked was still in its fledgling stage—a stage from which it would, in fact, never quite fully emerge—when my friend Natalie Cox told me that I should check out what was going on down in Olympia. She thought, rightly, that I might feel a musical kinship with some of the bands coming out of there: Bikini Kill, Bratmobile, Heavens to Betsy, and others. So, though it felt slightly traitorous up in Seattle, I started seeking out K Records singles and sending away for the cassettes these Olympia bands were releasing. I bought the 7-inch compilation *There's a Dyke in the Pit*, which featured the Bikini Kill song "Suck My Left One." I also purchased the first eponymous Kill Rock Stars compilation that had the Bikini Kill song "Feels Blind." I remember being deeply struck by the lyrics: "Look what you have taught me / Your world has taught me nothing," and "As a woman I was taught to always be hungry . . . We could eat just about anything / We might even eat your hate up like love."

To me, that perfectly summed up being a young girl. It was the first time someone put into words my sense of alienation, the feeling that all these institutions and stories we'd been taught to hold as sacred often had very little to do with my own lived experiences. I had already been listening to punk and had related to storytellers like Joe Strummer and Paul Weller, but hearing Bikini Kill was like having someone illuminate my world for the first time. Here was a narrative that I could place myself inside, that I could share with other people to help explain how I felt, especially at a time when I was a shy and fairly inarticulate teen. I could turn the volume up on their songs and that loudness matched all my panic and fear, anger and emotions that seemed up until that point to be uncontrollable, even amorphous. Bikini Kill's music really gave a form, a home, and a physicality to my teenage turmoil. Eventually I was able to harness that tumultuousness, build on it and make it my own. It's hard to express how profound it is to have your experience broadcast back to you for the first time, how shocking it feels to be acknowledged, as if your own sense of realness had only existed before as a concept. I felt like I could step inside something; it was a revelation.

More than they influenced my style of playing, Bikini Kill helped to embolden me. I still see music as an act of defiance as much as it is an act of celebration. A lot of my ideas about earning it and owning it come from Bikini Kill's early influence on me.

I feel very lucky that Bikini Kill came first. By the time I was playing in Sleater-Kinney, a lot of those early battles—for space, for respect, for recognition within the context of punk and indie music—had already been fought. We were ultimately recognized as a band, not just as a female band, and that is a luxury that cannot be overstated. A certain kind of exhaustion sets in from having to constantly explain and justify one's existence or participation in an artistic or creative realm. What a privilege it must be to never have had to answer the question "How does it feel to be a woman playing music?" or "Why did you choose to be in an all-female band?" The people who get there early have to work the hardest. Bikini Kill weren't the first—they had predecessors and influences—but they carved, tore, and clawed out a space in music for which I am very grateful.

I had started running away from home in high school—nothing dramatic, simply leaving for a few days with no intention to return. Sometimes I told my father, other times I did not. Late at night, I'd put the car in neutral and push it out of the garage with the engine off. Halfway down the driveway, I'd start the motor. My moods and my whereabouts went undetected for the most part, and I think in part that is why I didn't want to be around—I felt unseen and thus sought out visibility elsewhere. I took comfort in the families of various friends. I was appreciative of the attention they gave me, the kindness. I spent Easter with one friend by default, as I had spent Saturday night at her house and woke up to the Sunday holiday. For my best friend Katie's mother I did chores, I vacuumed and dusted. I loved how normal these lives felt so much that I was willing to perform tasks I would only do for my own father after much resistance. I watched movies and sat around dinner tables discussing art and politics, inserting myself into conversations and dynamics so that I could sense what it might feel like to be held accountable, to be required to show up. I practiced being a daughter, a sister, someone who had a role and traditions. I existed half in my own family and half in others. I was such a frequent resident at Katie's house that her mom asked my father if I would switch to a private school senior year; she feared Katie wouldn't go otherwise. I applied and got in. I felt like no one was really looking out for me, that I was marginal and incidental. I compensated by being spongelike, impressionable, and available to whatever and whoever provided the most comfort, the most sense of belonging. I was learning two sets of skills simultaneously: adaptation—linguistic and aesthetic—in order to fit in, but also, how to survive on my own.

When it came to applying to college, discussing the options with my father, it all took on a desultory shape. Despite my being accepted at Lewis & Clark, it turned out we couldn't afford it. I was stuck with my backup choice. I really didn't want to go to Western Washington University. I had no plan, and I left for the northern part of the state knowing only that I would not be there long. Departing for a departure. Nevertheless, I went through the motions. I set up my dorm room inside a building that resembled a Travelodge: entrances on the outside, concrete, unglamorous, and institutional. My favorite thing about Western was the meal card, a fact that began to show up on my increasingly rounded cheeks.

Perhaps it was my lack of commitment that prevented me from making friends. I spent my days listening to records and trying to ingratiate myself to a roommate named Aimee who had grown up in Olympia. In my vision of Olympia, it was mythical. It was Paris or Berlin in the '20s, it was the Bloomsbury group, it was the cradle of civilization. I sensed Olympia would be my salvation, where I needed to end up. It was also tiny. I assumed that every denizen of that town was a young punk,

walking around with a bag full of 7-inch singles and a fanzine, and in
a band.

But Aimee had never heard of these bands from Olympia. So she
graciously let me proselytize to her about her own hometown, a town
she was likely relieved to have departed, off to bigger and better things.
I regaled her with tales of indie labels. I played her Heavens to Betsy and
Bikini Kill cassettes and KRS compilations. She tried to be helpful, filling in geographical gaps in my knowledge while I filled in musical ones
in hers. Aimee became an ersatz lifeline for me, a temporary and tenuous pathway to where I wanted to go. It was a pitiful and one-sided
friendship, and one I probably remember with more fondness and importance than she ever will. She was a placeholder for me, just some
unwitting kid from Olympia who would serve as a stand-in for my
dreams and aspirations.

I went to a show in the cafeteria where a local band played a cover of
the Go-Go's "Our Lips Are Sealed." I remember seeing the guitarist
walk around campus the next day, and I was filled with wonder. I wanted
to be someone who had that power to drift in and out of people's imaginations, who could be bigger than mere human form, a surface upon
which others could project their longings. I needed other people's outward manifestations of self to help me realize who I could be.

A girl at Western named Andie—lumbering and slouched, but way
more motivated and less self-conscious than I was—immediately got
involved in the radio station, wanting to bring bands to the school. In
that fall of 1992, she brought Mudhoney to Western. We learned that
there was going to be a surprise guest, and that the guest would be Nirvana. They would "open" the show.

When Nirvana took the stage, they played in front of an audience
that didn't really expect or deserve their presence—which was proba-

bly all they had hoped for at that moment. I, of course, completely took for granted the fact that they likely felt lucky they could still surprise anyone, that they could sneak onto a stage and play a normal show, that they could open for friends in a small college town in their home state, that they could pretend to still just be some normal guys. I took for granted that set, the ease and exuberance of it. They played mostly off *Nevermind*, just three people with the best songs you've ever heard, scrappy and guttural and really loud. And as openers for Mudhoney you could really hear the context from which all this was happening: chainsaws making sonic carvings, hollowed-out selves amplified and discordant. There was some thread of sweetness underneath, a melodic sense that hit you in the back of the throat and made you want to raise up a weary, tentative fist, hoping that gesture would mark you as having been found, or ready to no longer feel lost.

And even though it was Nirvana—*Nirvana*, playing a secret show at my school—the best musical moment at my time at Western was yet to come.

Fliers went up for Bikini Kill, Heavens to Betsy, and Mecca Normal. The three bands were coming to play at the Showoff Gallery in downtown Bellingham.

I had been listening to Heavens to Betsy every day. They had a six-song cassette that intrigued me in a way nothing before had. It was a combination of Corin Tucker's voice and the lyrics. The beautiful parts were edged in disgrace and disgust; it bordered right on ugly the whole time. The singing was louder than it needed to be—did she even need a mic? The music was rudimentary, the drums like an uneven stagger, a determined but ungraceful late-night walk home, the guitar or bass playing just a pattern that repeated until it was an incision—but it was the voice that really cut through. The voice asked to be listened to but it did not beg or plead, it dared and challenged, it confronted but needed no reply from the listener. Any sadness was also defiant: it was not the wail of mourning but of murder. And there was so much I wanted to destroy.

I went to the Heavens to Betsy show with Aimee. A sign on the door announced that Bikini Kill had canceled on account of a family illness. It didn't matter, I'd still see Heavens to Betsy. *The Los Angeles Times* had sent a reporter and a photographer to cover the show. At the time, Riot Grrrl was a movement that the mainstream press was desperate to understand. News outlets continually attempted to infiltrate the underground, never to really get a handle on it, only serving to mischaracterize its impact.

Heavens to Betsy was a wolf in sheep's clothing: two small women who took up very little physical space on a stage. Typically when a two-person band performs live, they find ways of compensating for their diminutive population via aesthetic amplification and augmentation. They surround themselves with a cityscape of amplifiers; they use drum risers and lighting to create formidable shadows, a landscape of giants; they find ways to add a sense of largeness. But Corin had only her hand-made guitar that her father had helped build. It was a crude piece of machinery painted matte black, and it looked like a home appliance that had been melted down in a fire. And she played with the tiniest of amps, an orange Roland cube with one speaker, the entire thing the size of a carry-on suitcase. No pedals, no tuner. She was accompanied by Tracy Sawyer, the drummer and occasional bass player Corin had dragged along with her to Olympia from their childhood hometown of Eugene, Oregon. Tracy backed up Corin tentatively but proudly, stubbornly, the way a younger sibling would, with a secret and shy courage. The noise they made in Heavens to Betsy was vicious and strange. It completely changed one's notion of what it meant to be powerful on-stage. It was not about strength in numbers nor in size. It had nothing to do with volume. It was about surprise. It was about knowing you were going to be underestimated by everyone and then punishing them for those very thoughts.

They took themselves seriously, too. It was a strident show. Eventually Corin was able to bring her sense of humor about the world and about herself into her music. But when you're part of an early movement like she was with Riot Grrrl—where she had to create a space for herself and for her audience, where every show felt like a statement, where before you could play and sing you had to construct a room, one you'd be respected in, wouldn't get hurt in, a space that allowed for or even acknowledged stories that hadn't been told before, about sexual assault, sexism, homophobia, and racism, and then, musically, you have to tear that very space down—there's not a lot of room for joking around. There is a direness in the construction of safety, in the telling of theretofore untold stories. I was really intimidated by those Heavens to Betsy shows. I thought, *These people are so cool and so not funny.* I knew not to kid around or make some crass, sarcastic comment because, well, these people will fuck you up. Heavens to Betsy came across as the most serious of their peers. You stood up, you listened, and you were quiet. They were like really loud librarians. And as the audience, you better shut the hell up because you're in the library of rock right now.

When Heavens to Betsy finished their set, I walked up to Corin. I told her I wanted to drop out of Western and move to Olympia. She said I should do that, and soon. It felt like an order. She had a spiral notebook and I wrote down my address and told her to keep in touch. Knowing my days in Bellingham were numbered, especially now that my departure had been ordained by this singer I admired, I gave her my father's address back in Redmond. Now I *had* to leave; what if Corin reached out to me and I wasn't there to receive her beck and call?

My first real band, Excuse 17, would eventually tour the United States with Heavens to Betsy. The audiences were very earnest. And due to the political nature of Heavens to Betsy, it felt like a real dialogue between band and audience, almost like they were bringing a lecture into town. After the shows Corin would spend a lot of time talking to audience members about issues or even objections they had with her music, or with certain lyrics, or with punk or indie music in general. I'd see someone finger-pointing, and I would be annoyed for her. But Corin would always be grateful for the interaction.

For me, that tour, the music, the whole punk scene, felt very made up as it went along. There was a malleability to it as we vacillated between, experimented with, or claimed identities. If someone didn't feel included, if someone felt marginalized, they would form their own band, write their own fanzine, or just call you out on what they deemed racist or classist, sizeist, sexist, body-ableist. For a movement that professed to grant one a sense of belonging and solidarity, we were often made aware of our differences. In the span of a single show, or in the reading of a fanzine or the lyric sheet of an album, one's own experiences could be publicly validated in one instant and then invalidated the very next. There was a real power struggle to find a coalescence and to acknowledge commonalities in our disparities. We wanted to protect one another, to be inoffensive, inclusive, aware of our own shortcomings and faults, to improve and evolve, to make radical changes. Yet there was so much pressure on this single indie and punk movement, one that clearly couldn't address all forms of personhood or inequality.

I should acknowledge that I am so grateful for Corin, who, coming up through Riot Grrrl, was never afraid to be unpopular in her beliefs.

Who worried so little about what others thought. Because of her I could applaud from the sidelines, I could apply my own analysis to the situation from a safe distance. In our years writing songs together, Corin could make the mess and I could figure out what it meant and what significance it held. It was a good balance. She was plainspoken and trenchant. She could write lyrics to "Dig Me Out" and those three words could tell you everything you needed to know about the feeling of smallness, of being held back, of such a basic desire to tear even a fraction of light into any form of darkness we're dealt with. I could grapple with titles like *Wilderness* or *Moonless* for our seventh record and Corin could just say, "What about *The Woods*?" and that was that. *The Woods*, of course! It doesn't merely describe something—it *is* something.

When I dropped out of Western and moved back home with my father, he seemed certain I had ruined my life, that I'd never get back to college, have a job, or amount to anything. He was flummoxed by my indecision and lack of drive. I, on the other hand, was ready to test whether my increasingly thorny disposition could puncture the soft padding of my suburban environs. One catch to that plan—a cliché one, no less—was that I still needed my dad's help. (Like a lot of middle-class kids, I needed my punk rock and rebellion underwritten by my parents.) I wanted to go to Evergreen State College, not so much to study as to have a valid excuse to be in Olympia. My father agreed to let me live at home as long as I left for college in the fall as planned.

The interim was difficult. I worked my first real jobs. One was for a catering company that delivered meals to office parks. I'd wheel a cooler full of salads and sandwiches that had been prepared in the wee hours of the morning in a nondescript warehouse into an office lobby, where the receptionist would make an announcement over the PA: "Deli girl is here." Who was this deli girl to whom she was referring? Oh, it was me. I figured out a way of manipulating the numbers so that I could take a chicken salad and a piece of lemon pound cake home at the end of the day. It was a tiny, ineffectual "fuck you" to "the man." The woman who trained me had a perky sales routine that she passed on to me in order to boost my numbers. (She also suggested I remove my nose ring, or at the very least clean it on occasion.) She'd tell her customers that she had some pound cake "here" and "here," pointing at each of her thighs. I laughed at the middle-aged-lady aspect of it until I myself gained ten pounds and was humbled by being college-aged but clearly not in school. Here I was delivering meals-on-wheels to people my age who were already working their way up the corporate ladder. And even though I had never imagined myself on the corporate ladder, I had also never pictured myself peddling tuna fish on sourdough to those who were. So I quit.

Next I got a job in telemarketing. I worked for a company that helped college kids get summer jobs on cruise ships or fishing up in Alaska. They didn't actually help anyone get anything, they simply sold a book with a list of phone numbers and addresses. I was pretty great at reading the script into the phone, deviating from it only enough to add my own flair and personal charm. I was making $10 an hour and got promoted to the mail room. There I gave myself daily paper cuts that I used as reminders, witchy whispers to myself letting me know this was only temporary.

What I wanted was to play music. My friend Jana, whom I had met in a high school chemistry class and who had played bass in Born Naked, was now at the University of Washington. She and I would go out on band auditions, separately or together, showing up at houses where purple-haired punks took us to their basement and we'd run through Agent Orange songs ("Bloodstains"). I never felt scared for my life, only nervous not to play well, self-conscious about my youth and that my preppiness would show through. Everyone wanted to have a girl punk band, especially with L7, Hole, 7 Year Bitch, Lunachicks, and Bikini Kill all getting attention. I auditioned for a band called Not My Son, which pretty much sums up the moniker trend of the time. In high school I had jammed with guys and had been doing a fair bit of auditioning for bands that were co-ed, but I was more excited about the Olympia scene and its kin, about Heavens to Betsy and Bratmobile, about Tiger Trap and Autoclave, about bands like Kreviss with eight girls in it, about Slant 6—I wanted to have a girl gang.

Jana and I would place "musician wanted" ads in *The Rocket*, Seattle's music weekly. We were searching for a drummer and a singer. People would reply to the ad and we would go to their houses to audition them. I don't know why we didn't make people come to us—perhaps because we didn't have a drum kit—but it felt like we were enacting some strange variation of the traveling salesman. We would bring our amps and our guitars and set up in strangers' basements or living rooms, unloading our wares and doing a musical sales pitch.

Arriving at each house was the ultimate blind date: no pictures had been exchanged, no MP3s sent over the computer. It was often obvious the second the woman would answer the door that we didn't have mutual taste in music. Despite this, there was a hopefulness to the process. I'd think, You only like the Indigo Girls and you have your old dreadlock taped to the wall—but we're both women so this should work out just fine. There was, for example, the carton-of-cigarettes-a-day couple with the husband acting as a proud stage dad, talking up his wife the whole time. The woman was about twenty years older than us, worn-in skin with bleached hair, gray roots on display. She was squat and tough, a 4 × 4 of a human. She sang her heart out over our rudimentary three-chord song, channeling Janis Joplin and Ann Wilson, with a croak and ache of experience that we were years from knowing. Her husband stood next to her during the entire audition, president of a one-person fan club, rooting for her (and his) big break. As if two kids from the suburbs, more Bert and Ernie than Lennon and McCartney, were going to take this woman to the top of the charts.

We were so often mismatched; the tryouts were a heartbreaking and humbling experience. Every audition was *American Idol* in miniature, dreamers meeting up with other dreamers, pinning our hopes on the least likely, yet always undeterred.

Even then, I could still appreciate the moment of simply making sounds with a group of people. There is another place you go to in those instances, and it feels vast, refreshing, like you're creating your own air to breathe. And even though it's never going to happen again and there's a palpable sense of mediocrity, there's still a connection that you wouldn't have otherwise, to the sound, to the people. I think for those reasons I've always been able to appreciate (but be simultaneously heartbroken by) bar bands and karaoke—you witness the playing or the singing and you know that just being up there, engaged in a momentary artifice, a heightening of self, is sometimes enough to get by, to feel less worn down by, less withered by life. Sometimes it's everything.

7 Year Bitch, a rock band of all women, were the heroines of the Seattle scene in the '90s. They were equally as tough as the rock dudes and they seemed like they partied just as hard. 7 Year Bitch's music was fierce and growly, and their onstage personas—in particular lead singer Selene Vigil's—were as amped as their songs. They weren't as catchy or punk-based as their Olympia counterparts, but I felt an affinity with them because of their geographical proximity to me, like I owed them that loyalty. They exemplified the Seattle sound of the era: their songs had a rough, unadorned quality, as if they were scraped from tree bark. Stefanie Sargent, their young and talented guitarist, had recently died of a heroin overdose. I had no relationship with drugs, nor any idea how one could journey down a dark path only to dig further into blackness; when she overdosed in 1992, the year I had graduated from high school, her death felt like a distant, imperceptible loss, a hollowing that only later I realized would grow each time a musician died.

One week, scanning *The Rocket*, as I always did, searching for a band to join, for an ally across the bridge in Seattle, for some way out of Redmond, I came across an ad that read simply: "Girl guitarist wanted, no wanky solos." That is me, I thought. After all, I don't even know how to play a solo, let alone a wanky one. I called the number, and Elizabeth Davis from 7 Year Bitch answered.

I couldn't believe someone who I thought was fairly famous would be placing an ad in a local paper, that she could just be a normal person on the other end of the line. I shook and talked too fast and laughed when there weren't any jokes. Here's how I remember it: I'm lying on my twin bed in my dad's house on some highly flammable two-tone comforter.

ELIZABETH: You play guitar?
CARRIE: Ha ha ha ha. Yes.
ELIZABETH: It's raining out.
CARRIE: I know. Ha ha ha.

I was hysterical.

I told her I loved 7 Year Bitch and then I rattled off a bunch of Olympia bands that I liked—Bikini Kill, Bratmobile, Beat Happening—until I worried that I sounded too biased toward the town south of us, and then I heard the word "Soundgarden" come out of my mouth. I offered to learn their songs and come over to audition. For the next two days I sat in my room listening to their "Lorna" 7-inch over and over, memorizing the parts, already imagining myself up onstage, on tour, with a new life and new friends. Learning a song from a 7-inch is not easy. There is no pausing, no replay, just picking up and putting down the needle again and again.

I drove with Katie, my best friend from high school, in my Honda CVCC. It was a death-on-wheels clown car, blueberry-round, stick shift, seats covered in lamb's wool, updated with an Alpine stereo. We went over the 520 bridge to Seattle and into the Queen Anne neighborhood where Elizabeth lived. My outfit was a classic suburban impersonation of a more urbane look: cutoff jeans with a slight pleat at the top paired with an oversized Hanes T-shirt I took from my dad's dresser. I also wore one of my father's suit vests, which swung out from my body like saloon doors. Worst of all was that I had a green J.Crew baseball cap atop my head that I inexplicably wore backward. In a momentary fit of self-consciousness and doubt (and I am relieved that I can write this), I removed the hat before I got out of the car. I was eighteen. Katie waited in the parking lot. I brought my guitar in with me in case Elizabeth might want to spontaneously jam or wanted a more formal audition.

Elizabeth answered the door in something black, a color so obvious and easy, a shorthand for cool. Why hadn't I thought to wear black? I looked clean-cut in comparison, and like I might be there to deliver pizza or ask her to save the whales. I was then offered a beer. It was midday. I was at the age where I only drank to get drunk and alcohol was something I still snuck from my dad, usually a blend of five different alcohols skimmed from the liquor cabinet and then diluted with Coke inside a giant plastic cup from a fast-food restaurant giveaway. Sitting around sipping a beer in the daylight felt wrong, and I wasn't even sure I liked beer if it wasn't being poured down my throat, circumventing my taste buds via beer bong.

I sank into a couch, which only made me feel smaller and even less capable. Elizabeth talked a little about Stefanie and the day of the funeral. It was odd to be privy to what I considered a private matter, or a public one that I'd only read about in the papers—the death of a friend, a bandmate. I felt grown-up to be considered a temporary confidante but immature in the way I couldn't wait to tell my friends.

Then the singer, Selene, came over. This felt promising. I was being checked out, examined. Selene had a raspy voice and was all muscle shirt and sinew and messed-up hair. Suddenly, my oversized T-shirt seemed even bigger and whiter. There I was, a puffy cloud on a couch, surrounded by women who were so clearly thunder and lightning, and I wasn't even drinking a beer. I left knowing that they would never ask me to be in 7 Year Bitch.

Yet in my youthful ignorance and optimism I was determined to stay positive. I felt hopeful. That hope was quickly diminished when Elizabeth called me the next day and told me it wasn't going to work. She said I was too young and that the band played a lot of bar shows. I still didn't want to give up or let go; it didn't seem fair. I felt like this might be my only chance to be in a band, a real band. So, I did what any teenage girl would do: I wrote a letter wherein I compared myself to the Red Hot Chili Peppers guitarist John Frusciante. Frusciante had joined the Chili Peppers when he was eighteen or nineteen. And even though he was a genius guitar player, a true wunderkind, and I only knew a couple of chords, I felt like the comparison just might work. Not only was I likening myself to a virtuouso guitarist, but I was also displaying gumption and guts—at least that's what I thought. I would charm my way into this band, if not with my J.Crew outfits, then with savvy.

Unfortunately, I didn't end the letter there. Instead, I bared my soul. As in the letters I had written to soap stars and teenage heartthrobs in elementary school and junior high, I told Elizabeth about my entire life: how I didn't get along with my parents, about my mom leaving, the whole maudlin story. People think that the digital age and social networking sites like Facebook and Twitter nurture oversharing, but in 1992 there was nothing stopping me from treating any piece of paper like a personal diary. I wanted so badly to be taken to some special place, to be asked into a secret club that would transform my life. I felt like music was that club. And to see inside for a moment and then be asked to leave was devastating.

During the next few months I occasionally ran into Elizabeth at Seattle shows and music festivals like 107.7's End Fest. She was always kind to me but I had clearly become a pest. Later, when I knew what it felt like to carry the weight of your fans' aspirations, I would remember the way Elizabeth looked at me after I'd sent the letter: a look of pity, distrust, and weariness. There is a gulf of misunderstanding between musicians and their fans, and often so much desperation that the musician can't possibly assuage, rectify, or heal. You feel helpless and you feel guilty. With Sleater-Kinney fans I tried to be generous, but I soon grew uneasy. For a long while I could share nothing more than the music itself. I think I was too scared to be open with the fans because I knew how bottomless their need could be. How could I help if I was just like them? I was afraid I might not be able to lessen their pain or live up to their ideals; I would be revealed as a fraud, unworthy and insubstantial. The disconnect between who I was on- and offstage would be so pronounced as to be jarring. Me, so small, so unqualified.

In the early years of Sleater-Kinney, we played at Seattle's Crocodile Café. Elizabeth was at the show. By then, 7 Year Bitch had broken up. She came up to me, complimented my guitar playing, and told me she loved the band. Elizabeth didn't recognize me as the girl who had gone over to her house that day or written her an overly earnest tell-all letter. I was relieved that music had done exactly what I had always wanted it to do, which was turn me into someone else.

Jana and I had mostly given up on finding bandmates via classified ads. One night the Breeders were playing in Olympia at the Capitol Theater, so Jana and I drove down. We stood in the orchestra pit, crammed up against other kids, giddy with anticipation, wrapped up in that collective swell of appreciation and adoration. In front of us stood a group of girls with baby bangs and barrettes, yellow or black or red hair, and vintage glasses. Jana and I were awkward. She was nearly six feet tall with shaggy curls that she habitually tucked behind her ears with a bashful shrug. I had Manic Panic magenta hair and big cheeks, a nose ring that was constantly on the verge of infection, a thrift-store T-shirt from the boys' section paired with corduroys cut off at the bottom with scissors, no seam, frayed. We weren't exactly cool. We started talking to these girls and found out they lived in Seattle—a boon for us since befriending a bunch of Olympia kids would mean yet another thing that was out of our reach. By the end of the night, after singing along and matching Kim and Kelley Deal grin for grin, we had the phone numbers of Polly, Gilly, and Rachel.

It was early 1993 and I was floundering. My telemarketing office was in the University District near another branch of Cellophane Square, the record store I loved, and a guitar shop I could gawk at. Most of my work conversations consisted of people bragging that a friend of a friend knew the drummer in the Pixies or had lived in the same town as the singer from Toad the Wet Sprocket. I offered to be in a band with a cute and hip-looking woman whom I admired for her ability to pull off overalls, but she wasn't interested. I ate lunch in my car.

So meeting Polly, Gilly, and Rachel could not have come at a better time. It gave me a sense of purpose; it was inspiring, it was something to *do*, somewhere to *go*. Mostly Jana and I and the rest of the girls hung out at Polly's. She was living with her mom in the Wedgwood neighborhood of Seattle. Their house was small, underlit, cozily cluttered. We'd hang out what seemed like every night, dye each other's hair, put on makeup, listen to records, watch late-night music videos, get drunk, draw, lie around. It was languid, shapeless, and very sweet.

One night, after we'd all been hanging out for a few weeks, we were drinking some kind of saccharine liqueur, something you'd only drink if it were free—free as in stolen from one's parents. The flavor made for a woozy, treacly buzz. Polly suggested that we pass the drink mouth-to-mouth. It started like that, our mouths merely conduits, containers. The feeling was warm but still perfunctory. But somewhere in the middle of this contrived routine, this newfound alcohol-dispensing technique, was an ersatz kiss, another mouth. Soon I was centering in on the sensation, of the place where the lips touched, to see whether it felt good. And then the alcohol became secondary to skin. And then there was just kissing. It lasted hours, an expedition. It didn't feel revelatory, but it also didn't feel strange.

I woke up the next morning in my childhood bed and called Jana.

She felt sick, horrified. For her it had been an awakening, and she wanted to die. I was shut off from my body; I had barely thought about sexuality or longing. Up until this point, my sexual experiences had felt business-like or even transactional. A trade agreement with a neighbor wherein I'd give him a blow job and then later get something in return. That "something" never happened, by the way, though I am certain I didn't miss much. There was a party in high school where I spent the last hour essentially making out with the pimply back of a guy's neck who was sitting in front of me on the floor. I was too afraid to ask for more, or even suggest that he turn around. With female friends I had cuddled at sleepovers but never touched or reached out in any sort of romantic way. I hadn't been suppressing urges or denying my needs. I didn't feel like I had any, not corporeal ones. My journal entries from that time speak to depression and feelings of isolation, fears that a friend would leave, a sense that I had been responsible for my mother's departure and would therefore cause anyone I loved or needed to leave. I was still spending most of my time in my head. I was removed from my own feelings. Like so many aspects of my life up until that point, the only remarkable thing about that night was that it was a small version of letting go, which I sort of detested, and definitely feared.

The marathon makeout did bring to light that living with my dad and sister was proving problematic. In the brief time I had been in Bellingham, the two of them had somehow turned into bros more than anything resembling father and daughter. My sister's room was decorated with European beer bottles, and a La-Z-Boy was now parked in front of the living room TV. Stacey was mysteriously allowed to throw parties, and my dad's only social life seemed to revolve around her soccer games. I moved out of Redmond and into a cheap apartment in Seattle's Capitol Hill.

Now with all of us in the city, the five of us formed a band that we called Conspiracy A Go-Go. We practiced in the basement and recorded a four-track cassette tape so we could get a handful of shows in small bars—okay, in the *corner* of small bars, on a carpeted floor, during the day. Also, "handful" might be an exaggeration. We weren't very good. None of us could really sing, and the songwriting was rudimentary but not in a charming, purposely minimalist way. We didn't care that we were the musical version of a stick figure—it was more about feeling like we were doing something. It was a way of being around one another. By now the band consisted of two pseudo couples and a fifth wheel, "pseudo" meaning none of us would really admit to what was happening. We were like Fleetwood Mac without the sex or drugs or hair or songs.

Polly was friends with Calvin Johnson of K Records, so we got a show opening up for the Sub Pop band Codeine down in Olympia. This excruciating experience was how I learned about onstage sound and audio. I think people take for granted that there is any sort of manual for playing live. On this night, the first time I got onstage—a real stage —I had never used a proper PA or had anything other than the vocals miked. There was a speaker in front of me—a monitor, it turned out—but I had no idea that I would need to ask to get specific instruments in there. And for that matter, I didn't know what to even ask for, what would be important for me to hear to enable me to play the songs the way I knew them and to which I was accustomed. I had no idea that if I didn't get certain instruments in the monitor, I wouldn't be able to hear the other band members, that everything I knew about our songs would be dismantled and compartmentalized in a live setting. That depending on the shape of the venue and the stage, depending on the setup, I might only be able to hear myself. And that was the case. I couldn't hear the vocals or kick drum or bass. We were five people

playing a solo show simultaneously and not on purpose, not as a graduate school thesis or as an art project.

When people gripe about girls' rock camps or schools of rock, saying music, especially popular forms, can't be institutionalized or taught,
maybe part of that is true, but I always think about that night. How if
the process had been demystified, less of a private club or a secret code,
we wouldn't have sat in the dark theater after we played, watching
Codeine deliver a taut, deliberate set while we felt undeserving of having ever been onstage, blaming one another and ourselves, mad and
heartbroken.

PART 2
SLEATER-KINNEY

CHAPTER 6

SCHOOLED

I finally made my move to Olympia, nominally to return to school, in the summer of 1993. I was eighteen years old. Through writing to Tobi Vail, Becca Albee, and other girls I'd met via fanzines and Riot Grrrl, I managed to set up a sublet at a place called "The Haunted House," a.k.a. "The Punk House," a.k.a. "The Blue House." All the shared houses had names like that, often descriptors of their aesthetic, their proximity to a landmark or store, or referring to some talisman contained therein. Most residents knew little of the origin of their house's moniker. I was going to live in the room of Justin Trosper, who was heading out on tour with his band Unwound.

When I moved to Olympia I didn't really think of myself as a musician. I don't know if I would consider myself a musician now, not in the technical sense. I don't know much theory, I play by instinct and feel, I could probably get schooled by an eight-year-old on tonics and inversions. But back then, the word "musician" had a professional characteristic to it that would have made it even more alienating and anathema. Back then, I was still just a fan of music. And to be a fan of music also meant to be a fan of cities, of places. Regionalism—and the creative scenes therein—played an important role in the identification and contextualization of a sound or aesthetic. Music felt married to place, and the notion of "somewhere" predated the Internet's seeming invention of "everywhere" (which often ends up feeling like "nowhere").

Technically, in order to save face with my father, I moved to Olympia to attend Evergreen. But Olympia itself was a university I wanted to attend. Everything coming out of that scene had started to define me, or at least I wanted it to: the labels K Records and Kill Rock Stars, the bands, the fanzines, the people, the remnants of Riot Grrrl, the clothes. It was a world I was desperate to be part of. I wanted a new family of outlaws, of queers and provocative punks, of wit and sexiness. I had one trajectory and that was to get out: of Redmond, of my childhood, of my head. But I needed a place to land. I needed a place to take me in. It was both a calculated move and an aimless one. I possessed the force of a bullet, albeit one shot from a very shoddy gun.

I showed up to Olympia a wanderer. I had about two months until school started. I spent the first few weeks walking around downtown stopping in at the State Theater or thrift stores or the Martin apartments, places I knew people I wanted to be friends with worked or hung out. I lingered and muttered, I waited around. I was desperate to insert myself into situations, to learn, to observe. I was an archaeologist of sorts but I wanted to be a participant, to be connected and engaged. I was shy, which didn't help. Underneath that nervousness, however, I had a cunningness and intentionality, or at least a cluelessness that was intrepid enough to get the job done. I cared too much about what people thought but also not enough. I didn't mind that I was just hanging around. I didn't want to be discovered, I wanted to be part of the discovery.

I knew who all the players were, as if I were joining a sorority. I wanted to meet everyone. These musicians in punk bands, whom I'd read about in fanzines or seen mentioned in a record label newsletter, in *Maximum RocknRoll* or *Punk Planet*, were idols to me, larger than life. All my early school years vying for attention and status, a game I'd given up years before, I rechanneled and traded in for a different currency, a punk and indie rock currency, a marketplace of art and ideas. Here we dealt in arcane musical knowledge, in being completists, archivists, contrarians. We would go out on tours and come back with evidence from other scenes. It felt like reconnaissance in that way, like we were explorers and spies, an army.

I was scared my first summer in Olympia, flailing but strangely bold. I biked around town and rode skateboards in the Capitol parking lot. I drank too much malt liquor and cried on basement floors while bands played. I had unrequited crushes on girls, on entire bands, but mostly dated boys. More often than not I woke up hungover in friends' beds after a night of platonic spooning. I didn't care about setting down roots or having anything consistent. I wanted to be everywhere, talk to everyone. I was fumbling and barely formed, insecure and baby-faced, in polyester highwaters from the thrift store and used men's shoes with crummy soles and stretched, worn insides that my feet slid around in. I wore too-tight T-shirts and chunky belts, cut my own bangs uneven and jagged like an upside-down skyline, laughed too hard at everything, overshared.

A band called Huggy Bear from England descended upon our little town that summer. Afraid to fly, their guitarist, Jon Slade, stayed home. So Billy from Bikini Kill was the replacement. Huggy Bear were energetic, with a sophistication that not many of us in the Northwest had pulled off. They were cheeky—I don't know if that word has ever been ascribed to someone *not* from the United Kingdom. They conveyed drollness in their music; it was coy, sexy, and serpentine. I saw every show they played in the region, following them up to Seattle, driving down to Portland. I was a puppy dog for punk, and for Jo, who was probably the first girl I both really wanted *and* wanted to be: sunglasses-wearing, aloof, mysterious, with catchy riffs, her treble boosted so that it hissed through the songs. I drank so I'd have the nerve to keep hanging out, well past when I should have gone home. I tagged along on a trip to the ocean. I felt like a drifter. My heart hurt and I hated it.

Most nights I spent at basement punk shows, where we'd drink beer out of paper bags and sway like grass. I saw Karp and Unwound, Mary Lou Lord, Elliott Smith, Rancid, Jawbreaker, Drive Like Jehu. It seemed a touring band came through Olympia every night. Bands that would never play small towns now stopped there to hang out and fraternize with their friends in the local scene. They dropped in to home recording studios to make a 7-inch, they partied, they crashed on floors and hooked up with their Oly girlfriends. Sometimes they'd play multiple nights. Bigger bands like Beck or Stereolab would play the backstage of the Capitol Theater, the stage set up so performers would have their backs to the seats and the balcony while the audience stood in what is usually everything behind the curtain. It sounded horrible, as most of the noise escaped up into the main room. But I didn't think much at all about fidelity or professionalism, just about experience, about witnessing, about watching the way someone else danced or moved. All the music was still very much a mystery, how it all cohered. I discerned very little between good and bad bands, popular or obscure. *Every* band was good. Every player had a purpose, was standing his or her ground, contributing, making a sound. Any band was worth buying a single from, supporting, dancing along to. I could find appeal in the sway of a bass player or the cocky head bop of a drummer, in the musculature, in the posturing, in the daring hint of sexiness that you'd never witness offstage, in a glance or glare, in the reveal of a fang, in a singer's spit in the act of screaming, in sweat forming on a chest or hairlines, in a dropped pick somehow reclaimed mid-song, in a smile between two band members. I saw merit and beauty in it all—and if not beauty, then purpose, or at least just a way of positing yourself in the world, standing in one spot and being heard, etching your name somewhere, even if it disappeared shortly after. But at the time it all felt permanent, the most permanent and concrete thing I'd ever felt, and I was surrounded. Mostly what I felt was that I wanted to do that, too.

But there was also, of course, the actual college. Olympia's communal spirit possessed an almost utilitarian mind-set, where our worth was measured by the happiness and progress of the whole. Not coincidentally, almost all of us in the music scene had gone to the Evergreen State College. Founded in the late 1960s, Evergreen favors experiential learning. Grades are qualitative and it is unnecessary to declare a major. At the core of the Evergreen pedagogy is the seminar, wherein students and their professors engage in polemical discussion. The seminar doesn't adhere to the more hierarchical lecture format; instead, it allows for a collective sharing, examination, and deconstruction of ideas.

I often suspected the Olympia music scene would not have existed outside of this influence. Though it mimicked other punk scenes in its anti-corporate stance, it was a community in dialogue with itself. The rhetoric surrounding and about the scene was tantamount in importance to the labels, the bands, the musicians. We operated as if in a constant seminar. Everything was mutable and vulnerable to critique; it was all a shared experience. Bands felt like collective entities, with everyone having a say in what the music meant, calling out each other on wrong steps—an exhausting endeavor but one that built a special and sometimes frustrating insularity. Olympia was the quintessential "in" crowd versus "out" crowd. Visiting bands were either in awe or felt thoroughly snubbed. Though there was indeed a certain amount of snobbery, I think it was that our interactions had been codified, partly as an identifier, but also by necessity. The claustrophobia of small-town dynamics makes for new rules in terms of greetings and salutations; privacy and alone time were often only achieved by looking down as you walked along the streets. This mode of self-preservation and insularity can be off-putting to visitors.

Playing music seemed like the easiest way to communicate with my friends in Olympia. Everyone, it seemed, was not in one band, but in two or three. It would have been easier to count the people *not* in bands. And the music's value wasn't always based on technical acuity—there was a lot of deliberate underachieving and subversion. Bands like Witchypoo wore helmets and had transient members; they did spoken word over barely tuned guitars. The premium was not always on singing but on earnestness, sincerity croaked out or yelped, love songs made tart and less trite because they were voiced in a slant, slope, or scream. Angst compensated for everything. Some Velvet Sidewalk, Kicking Giant, Karp, duos and trios that sang as if every line was punctuated with an exclamation point. It was the sound of a magnified muttering, loud and distorted. Some bands possessed a purposeful clumsiness, while others couldn't help teetering, but any inelegance masked something sharper. Scissors and knives.

I started playing with Becca Albee and CJ Phillips. We called our band Excuse 17. Becca was a writer and artist from Portland, Maine, who was going to school at Evergreen. She lived in the Martin apartments, which were the veritable *Melrose Place* of Olympia, a punk rock dormitory right in the center of town. Becca had been kind to me from the beginning. She seemed eager to forge a musical project with someone new in town, someone not already associated with another band. We both played guitar, and in typical Oly style, a bass player seemed an unnecessary addition. Becca had a good sense of melody and of creating character and story in songs, which there wasn't a lot of in the first-person, sometimes stark narratives of the Riot Grrrl bands. She listened to Elvis Costello and Throwing Muses and had a slightly more sophisticated palate than I did. I was always seeking a kindred desperation in music, whereas Becca possessed a sturdiness that allowed her to appreciate the more refined. I was anxious to pour my guts out, and many of my songs with Excuse 17 are a sonic and lyrical purging, a caged animal who upon release heads straight to the recording studio. Fortunately, Becca's intelligence tempered my screeches and squawks, and I managed to learn about cowriting, about arrangement, about restraint. Then there was CJ, who was from the Seattle suburb of Federal Way. He had an affect of sensitivity that was so common among the young men I knew as to be pro forma, this gentleness a phase many men entered or adopted as they tried to navigate the matrifocal environs of Olympia.

Compared with our counterparts, I think Excuse 17 felt relatively normal and nonthreatening. We were well-mannered, thoughtful, and square. At one point early on, Becca and I tried to stir up drama by saying we had made out on a weekend getaway, just to add a sense of salaciousness or myth. No one cared or believed us.

Excuse 17 made two records, and we all saw the country for the first time together. We were treated a little like junior varsity players—not good enough to be on the real team, but by being around we helped make the whole program seem legitimate. We went on a tour opening for Heavens to Betsy, where Corin and I watched each other play every night and developed a mutual admiration. Before our show at the famed CBGB, a friend drove Corin and me to the Empire State Building, where we rode an elevator up to the observation deck, looked out over a luminous and pulsating city, then descended back into the grid, returning to the club only a few moments before we needed to play. (We missed out on seeing our opening act, a singer whom we were told was too afraid to look at the audience. Nevertheless, CJ said her voice and songs were stunning, that they'd made him cry. He proudly showed us the 7-inch single he'd purchased, the first one released by this artist, who went by the name Cat Power.)

If nothing else, those early tours with Becca and CJ allowed me to watch bands and musicians from other cities play over and over again, night after night. I would watch Richard Baluyut of Versus and Christina Billotte of Slant 6 play guitar. Richard really split apart and arpeggiated the chords, like a dour version of R.E.M.'s Peter Buck. Christina's guitar tone was garage-y with distinction—not just a growl, it had teeth. And the relationship between her singing and playing really influenced me, the way she sang her guitar lines, made them a unified theme and then broke them apart. She had a great voice, cool and insouciant. I wasn't a good singer but I had a decent grasp of melody, so I tried to approximate the notes.

By the time Excuse 17 was ending, my guitar-playing style was getting closer to what early Sleater-Kinney would sound like and what I ended up bringing to the table with Corin. Since neither Excuse 17 nor Sleater-Kinney had a bass player, the trick was finding a way of filling out the sound, making sure it had a depth and low end. We weren't into a lo-fi trebly noise; we weren't interested in accentuating or exaggerating the fact that we didn't have a traditional bass player. We wanted to sound like a full rock band. I suppose it's strange that our solution wasn't to simply add a bass player, but we didn't. Living in Olympia, we had lost perspective on what a traditional group looked or sounded like; band configurations were abnormal, either multi-limbed or conspicuously amputated. Additionally, neither Corin nor I were interested in playing too many bar or power chords. So my chords were half formed; I was always trying to leave room for Corin. My entire style of playing was built around somebody else playing guitar with me, a story that on its own sounds unfinished, a sonic to-be-continued, designed to be completed by someone else.

Corin had been the sole songwriter in Heavens to Betsy, and the only other instrument in her band was drums. She had never played with another guitarist before. But she and Tracy had not approached the combination of guitar and drums from a conventional standpoint either, largely due to lack of experience and skill, and it made for a distinct sound. Neither settled nor locked into each other, they were like two soloists, the drums an insistent knock on the door while Corin played by herself in another room. By the time we were in Sleater-Kinney together we had both—and perhaps unintentionally—developed ways of playing that were very compatible with each other, each having made minute adjustments in our other bands, each used to compensating yet unafraid of space or discord. I think part of the uniqueness of our sound is that we rarely land on a basic chord—the music stays somewhere in between, it's always not quite right, which of course can sound more right than anything, or at least like nothing else.

In Heavens to Betsy, Corin had always tuned her guitar to her own voice. So it was completely arbitrary that when she plugged into a tuner one day in an attempt to coordinate our tuning, her guitar happened to be in C-sharp. We never thought to alter it. It's one and a half steps below standard tuning, which creates a sourness, a darkness that you have to overcome if you're going to create something at all harmonious and palatable. So even when we're getting toward a little bit of catchiness or pop sheen, there's an underlying bitterness to it. The tuning also forced Corin to sing differently—it pushed her into her higher registers, into a wailing, the outer edges.

Corin was small with large eyes and an intense stare, like she was in a state of both pre-grudging and pre-judging. In reality, she was neither. She was kind, thoughtful, and fiercely loyal, though you would not want to cross her. She lived on the top floor of a duplex in the South Capitol neighborhood in Olympia. It was a studio apartment with sloped ceilings, the kitchen the size of a closet. Using a label maker, she had printed out words and phrases and stuck them on various household objects. It was part feminist art show, part lecture hall, part house of mirrors. You'd walk around the apartment and be confronted with words like "Racist" affixed to a can of Calumet baking powder. I'm not sure why she didn't just avoid the brand, but I suppose if you're in a period of continual confrontation, why stop at yourself. Then you'd see the cheap full-length mirror leaning against the wall, plastic frame broken and bent, and the words "You Are Beautiful" on a sticker across the top. Even when in the name of self-affirmations, the label maker made the words ominous and jarring. I always felt like I was bumping into walls in that apartment, the way those words would jump out at me like bogeymen when all I wanted to do was cook or check out my hair in the reflection. But I played along, learned from the process. I was under the tutelage of this strange world where you lived and examined all at once, questioned everything. It was school.

One day I got to my house and Corin had left me a message on the answering machine saying that we should name the band Sleater-Kinney. I knew "Sleater-Kinney" as the name of the road near which we had a practice space, a building not in Olympia but in the adjacent town of Lacey, which blistered with rundown chain stores and shoddy annual carnivals. At the time, I don't think we planned on doing much with this band; there was very little deliberation, no long list of potential names or backup ideas. Sleater-Kinney is a strange name—it sounds like a law firm or, as Lorrie Moore pointed out in one of her books, a hospital. We're none of those things, nor are we relatives of the Sleaters or Kinneys. But in the end the moniker could be whatever we wanted it to be. It could embody whatever and whoever we were.

Part in awe of the possibilities of this collaboration and my enthusiasm toward it, part unsure how seriously I should be taking all this, I tried to draw out the silliness in Corin. If we were going to really do this band, then I wanted to be myself around her, and "myself" was perhaps more goofy than I'd let on. I wanted to balance the seriousness with levity. I'd tell her made-up fairy-tale-like stories in order to entertain her, buy her trophies at thrift stores, or we'd sit around and listen to the operatic cheese of classic rock records like Supertramp or Boston, the latter of whose song "More Than a Feeling" we'd cover in our first recording sessions. We'd make out on her bed, no frame, just a mattress and box spring on the floor. We kept things waist-up, her suggestion, as she still had a boyfriend with whom she had an agreement that she could kiss members of the same sex. At nineteen, you can make out for hours, that goal-less, amorphous melting into someone else. Finally Corin broke up with her boyfriend. He acknowledged my so-called victory by giving me a photo he'd found of a boy sitting inside a basketball hoop. The note on the back read *You bagged my girl. —Dan.*

When I say that my experience with the music scene replaced traditional college experiences, that includes the sloppy, makeshift romantic aspects as well. There seemed to be a spin-the-bottle party about once a month. My first year in Olympia, I sat in the hallway of the Martin

The photo Corin's boyfriend Dan gave me.

apartments while kissing happened in rooms I was too afraid to enter. Eventually, I joined in. It felt like everyone was queer, that our sexuality and desires had less to do with our physical selves and more to do with music and art. Lust was part of the creative process, but the desire was often ambient. We did pair off into couples and date, but there was a fluidity to all things corporeal and quotidian. Perhaps because so many of us toured or played music, the hours were not structured around traditional industry or business, around mornings or lunch breaks. In those days, I hung out all the time, traveled in groups to group houses to eat group meals. We were amoebic. I was impressionable, open.

One year, K Records had a Valentine's Day party in the giant warehouse where they were headquartered. In the "Big Room" there was dancing. Across the hall, my friends Chad Quierolo (booking agent) and Julie Butterfield (public relations) were sharing an office, and they turned this smaller room into an exclusive, more intimate gathering. A spin-the-bottle game coalesced in the middle of the room, but soon spread out from the circle. Playing oldies from an AM radio station, we swayed and kissed. Mouths met in every corner, gooey and wet; gay boys kissed their best female friends, bandmates broke hard-and-fast rules, people in relationships put their promises on hold. It was sensual and disastrous. The next day I went over to Calvin Johnson's house, head pounding, stomach stormy. I wanted to see my friend Miranda July before she went back home to Portland. Her neck was covered in hickeys. Who are those from? I asked. You, she answered. For days after, everyone walked around with a cold.

I met Miranda in 1994, when Excuse 17 and Heavens to Betsy played at the punk rock venue known as 924 Gilman Street in Berkeley, California. Miranda was back in her hometown that summer, on break

Me and Miranda July at her parents' house. Berkeley.

from UC Santa Cruz. After playing our show, we stayed the night at her best friend's parents' house. Miranda came over in the morning, her hair cropped short and the color of a ripe blueberry. She was scrawny and angular, pale, with bright, piercing eyes, both delicate and dangerous. A rabid bunny. Within a few minutes of chatting with her in the kitchen, Miranda figured out that I was lying about my age. I wanted to seem more mature—twenty!!—when in actuality I was only nineteen. I think Miranda admired my gumption and I admired her directness. We've been friends ever since.

A few years later in Olympia, we were both dating older people who happened to have been a former couple. Miranda and I were living in crappy apartments, hers in Portland, the walls painted in garish circus stripes, mine in Olympia, carpeted and smelling as musty and stale as the thrift store from which all my furniture had come. Our respective dates lived in houses where they cooked and did laundry and had a second set of sheets. Miranda and I often wondered whether she and I shouldn't be together instead, but we never were. Instead, we forged a friendship based on shared ideas, adventures, mutual scrappiness, and curiosity. Miranda was already a polymath, recording spoken-word records and making short films. She ran a video distribution company called Big Miss Moviola (later called Joanie4Jackie). Girls from around the world would send her their short films; she would compile them and then release them like a visual chain letter. Sleater-Kinney played some shows with a group she was singing in called the CeBe Barnes Band. They had a variety of singers, and when it was Miranda's turn to be the front person, she seemed to emerge as if resurfacing from underwater, slithering and startled. Despite our loyalty to them, both Miranda and I felt slightly outside our own communities, but even early on there was a sense we'd be safe and emboldened as a team.

CHAPTER 7

SELF-TITLED

When I flew to Australia in the fall of 1994, I had never been overseas. It seems outlandish now, that I'd pick one of the most far-flung places on the map and endeavor to start a band there, but at the time it felt like a reckless sense of possibility.

Olympia is at the edge of a rain forest, and it's the grayest place I've ever lived. There's a dreariness to the town—it's a state capital, but it has a downtrodden feel. A combination of longshoremen, state workers, students. It feels like a transitional place. You always feel soaked. When I landed in Sydney at six a.m. after a fifteen-hour flight from L.A., the morning was already brightening.

Corin wouldn't land for another eleven hours, but I was met by Stephen O'Neil from the Cannanes, a person we knew only from correspondence—our host, our drummer, and hopefully our friend. His mouth had an upward tilt on one side that gave him a look of sweet eagerness. He picked me up in a navy blue van, and everything was novel to me, including the fact that we were driving on the wrong side of the road and it was spring. It looked like if San Diego were a country: exotic, dense flora and fauna, a mix of desert, beautiful spots of green and color, bright terraced houses, tropical sounds. I felt that first awareness that there's a whole set of species whose sounds and calls you've never heard—the wonder of realizing that people are growing up with an entirely different sensory experience from yours. This whole country seemed so shiny to me.

The night before we left home, it rained hard. Corin had moved out of her apartment, with no help from me—I was bidding farewell to a group of friends instead—and while attempting to open her door and wrangle a box, the door swung into her face and cut her above the eye. When Corin landed in Sydney, I'd had thirty hours of anticipation and excitement—we were going to start our band in this country!—while she'd had thirty hours for a deep resentment to congeal and solidify. She was cold and distant and had a swollen bruise above her eye, lashed by a freshly scabbed-over cut. Because it was too painful to put in her contacts, she was wearing glasses. All I could think to do when I first arrived in this foreign country was to buy trivial novelties that accentuated cultural differences. So, jet-lagged, I walked to the first corner store I saw to buy ketchup-flavored potato chips. I offered them to Corin, to no avail. I tried to cheer her up with ten bags of salty junk food in our room, where we rolled out our sleeping bags on the floor.

Corin and I had no money. We had traveler's checks and a $600 limit on my father's credit card. All this was to last nearly three months. We subsisted mostly on vegetarian pasties and soda and spent way too much energy trying to find the perfect school uniforms at charity shops in hopes that they might make good stage clothes. We had army-navy surplus backpacks so large it looked like we were giving free piggyback rides. We camped in the Blue Mountains, where a Gila monster invaded the grounds and we fled back to the city. With so much conspiring against us, most of it laughable and ridiculous, Corin warmed up to me again. We were on an adventure.

We had known the Cannanes' Stephen and Fran Gibson through letters, in the odd, endearing way that bands on like-minded labels formed an imitation cousinhood. We were welcomed into their home without much introduction or backstory, merely a shared interest in music—both making and listening—and a tacit acknowledgment that we knew some of the same people. Little vouching for one another was needed. Sight unseen, Stephen and Fran let us stay at their house for nearly a month. They cooked for us, made us tea in the afternoons, took us on ferry rides around the Sydney Harbor and to the aquarium. Corin and I were awed and grateful, though we felt a tad unworthy. We offered to do the dishes, not exactly certain how to compensate for their largesse or blatant display of adulthood, barely out of adolescence ourselves.

My and Corin's lack of preplanning about the entire trip made for moments of giddy spontaneity but also frequent errors in judgment and manners. One night I stuffed an entire plate of squid pasta into the waist of my pants. A week later I spent two days in bed after eating something called "Nut Meat" that I was certain had been pronounced "nutmeg" when I agreed to eat it. We kept forgetting to tell people we were vegetarians. On one occasion, my grandparents, concerned for our well-being on foreign soil, implored us to meet up with the cousins of their friends from back in Tucson. Thus it came to be that one afternoon Fela and Felix Rosenblum, along with their daughter and granddaughter, hosted Corin and me for a six-course lunch. Fela served us roast beef with an arm bearing her Holocaust tattoo. Neither Corin nor I had the nerve to refuse her offering, our choice of vegetarianism had unclear origins to begin with, but whatever they were, they felt paltry now. Neither Corin nor I have been vegetarian since.

There is something freeing in seeing yourself in a new context. People have no preconceived notion of who you are, and there is relief in knowing that you can re-create yourself. When you're entrenched in a community of people who know you, it's scary to proclaim wanting to be different and wanting to experiment. We went to the other side of the world to make our own sound. Usually this is a methodology you employ as a restart later in your career. We did it right up front. We traveled to a foreign country for our first record. We had to uproot ourselves, not because we were deep into career ruts, or didn't want to give credit to the places we had come from, but because we had no desire to sound like or emulate anything that had come before.

It was an extreme way to start, but I learned later on how hard it can become to unsettle yourself, to trip yourself up, and I think that's a good place to write from. It's important to undermine yourself and create a level of difficulty so the work doesn't come too easily. The more comfortable you get, the more money you earn, the more successful you are, the harder it is to create situations where you have to prove yourself and make yourself not just want it, but need it. The stakes should always feel high.

Stephen drummed for us in his living room as we began working on songs that would become our first record. Many of those earliest tunes didn't even have names. We called them "Last Song," "Slow Song," as if it were enough to merely have a song, a band. Titles? Who needed them. These were crude, blunt stabs with cookie-cutter structures. We didn't do any editing—the first idea was the only idea. There was no best, worst, or better, just raw attempts. We didn't modify or agonize. The chords and melodies were written, the structure was a container for what was less of a song and more of an attitude. We filled up these shapes with riffs and screams and yelps. I was not self-conscious about the writing process; I wrote rudimentary but melodic leads over Corin's crunchy three- or four-chord progressions. She sang whatever melody first came to her. The notion of simple or complex didn't really matter as much as sound. I guess you'd call that punk, but I also think it's just a matter of creating without the watchful eye of an audience or outside expectations in one's head. These weren't amazing songs, but they would form the foundation for our writing process, which was to create a single sonic sound with two guitars, two conversations. Corin was shy in person but confident and earnest onstage; I was introverted and overly cerebral, using playing as a means to get out of my head. Together we felt bold enough to be amplified.

What we lacked in deliberation we made up for in tenacity. We played guitar during the day and jumped onstage at night in pubs, opening for the Cannanes. Stephen wore ski goggles behind the drum kit, as if to make himself incognito. We played fast and out of tune; our sets lasted about four songs. I could never hear my voice in the monitor, whereas Corin flooded the system with her singing.

Despite my lack of sophistication or maturity, I was headstrong. My sense of possibility and certainty made me focused. I had blinders on. I was a sprinter—there were no long-term goals, I just knew I'd run as hard as I could in any situation. I'd learned that as an adolescent, to keep moving, to not be dragged down. The best word to describe it is "scrappy." I still feel that way today. Put me in a situation and I will find my way out of it or through it, I will hustle and scramble. I hate losing. Only later do I think about how it looks from the outside, and then I get stuck in a cycle of shame or anxiety—but in the moment, I rarely could see beyond it, I really could fight. I didn't think much about how it looked from the outside, or how I looked.

I strummed, I played. I let the music shake me and awaken me and then we'd be done, we'd leave the stage. And I'd return to being sheepish and stiff, overly concerned. The music really did feel like a cloak. And slowly I could wear that cloak—that confidence—in other settings, in conversations, at dinner parties or events, in school. (At Evergreen, I was too nervous to speak up in class. I knew what I wanted to say but didn't know how to interject or insert myself in a conversation. By the time I got up the nerve, my voice would be shaking, so even if I was saying something relatively innocuous or factual, I sounded like I was full of passion, emphatic, on the verge of crying. It was humiliating and my professors often noted my lack of participation.) It took a very long time to catch up with my performer self, to draw from that strength.

Corin had been in touch with her friend Ian, who was a fanzine writer and musician, and she'd asked him about finding someone to play drums for us in Australia. We knew Stephen was only a temporary solution. Ian put us in touch with Laura MacFarlane, who lived in Melbourne and played drums in the Sea Haggs. On what was essentially a blind date, we decamped for Melbourne, where we met our drummer. We hadn't actually listened to any recordings on which she played drums; again, verbal testimony and vouching were enough. Somewhere, we knew, we had a bandmate.

Laura had dimples and an infectious, conspiratorial laugh. She was a sprightly, elfin Scot who had grown up in Perth and played drums and guitar and sang. Unlike the ruddy surfer Australian stock, her hair was dark and her skin was light. She had a way of darting through a room.

Melbourne proved to feel much more akin to the Pacific Northwest than Sydney. Sydney was beautiful, but it felt more sophisticated. Melbourne had a grittiness that was relatable. The music scene was more politicized, more youthful. We stayed at the house of a girl named Sam, who wrote a zine called *Grot Grrrl*. Everyone seemed to have their own version of Riot Grrrl and their interpretation of punk rock feminism; these created a shorthand. It was reassuring to come across what felt like a network of people finding their voices for the first time. Those individual expressions formed a collective force, one that may have been lacking in refinement but was deeply sincere. That lack of composure made it even more unapologetic, and even if that gumption was compensatory, I think it's what scared people so much.

In those years I was in awe of the bravery I saw around me. I never quite felt brave myself then, but I watched a lot of fearless things happen. I could play at bravery in the songs, I could play at sexiness or humor, long before I could actually be or embody any of those things. Sleater-Kinney allowed me to try on so many roles. I think the music I both played and listened to, along with the unmasked, confessional writing in the fanzines, really created a vocabulary for me. Sometimes the works were smart or pithy, profound, poetic, and often they were really messy. But they formed a boundary and a foundation for a lot of girls who had been undone by invisibility, including myself. Girls wrote and sang about sexism and sexual assault, about shitty bosses and boyfriends, about fucking and wanting to fuck. They called out friends and relatives and bands and businesses, corporations and governments for what they felt were injustices. It was a very reactionary time. Each step felt like a landmine. On a personal level, and from those closest to you or in and around your community, you might get "zined" (the term for devoting pages of a fanzine to a person's perceived racist, sexist, classist, ageist, transphobic, whatever-ist behavior). I became acutely aware of myself as a political entity, but while the discourse felt important, necessary even, it also felt stifling. The perimeters felt unclear, almost like traps. Those bolder than I set forth unabashedly and were willing to be called out, but I stuck to watching it happen, on the periphery of the dialogue as an audience member and supporter, too scared to commit something treasonous. Only in the early songs was I willing to emulate that sort of naming and blaming, reclamation and wound-sharing. I didn't know how to really process those things in person.

Sleater-Kinney was never good at mythologizing. Earnest and unadorned, we were never self-effacing or apologetic, we just never thought to create a narrative other than the one we were living, never thought to heighten the story. The music was the only story. It really felt like a scratch or a scrawl—it didn't have an intentional design but you could read into it, you could wonder about it; the mystery was in the plainness, the starkness.

Sometimes I wish we'd had an elevated sense of mythos, that we'd come up in another scene, like 1970s New York with Richard Hell and Television, the New York Dolls and Blondie; or David Bowie and glam rock in England; or the Mods; or even just picking a dress code or a way of amplifying the sense of time and place. I remember trying to think of a different last name for myself: Rachel? Kinney? Always we just ended up back at who we were.

It was so Northwest. All about the music. The '90s had a monolithic feel, a sturdiness, realism as opposed to fantasy. In the punk scenes we came from, honesty was valued tantamount, or even more so than artistry. Even influencers and icons like Calvin Johnson or Kathleen Hanna—both much more aware of persona than anyone in my band— were still brought back down to earth by their engagement with politics and ethics. Once you have to explain, or overexplain, what you're doing, it's hard to be larger than life. Every time you have to talk about it, you feel smaller, more accessible perhaps, but certainly not mythic.

At shows, we often felt too brash, too bawdy. Corin's bravado was apt to court controversy, like the time in her hometown of Eugene, Oregon, when she yelled at a sound guy on my behalf that I couldn't hear my vocals and he got so fed up that he shut off the PA. We played anyway, and despite the futility and comedic potential, we even sang into the mics, miming our outrage to the audience. I wore business-casual clothes onstage, dressed up as if for a job, as if I were mocking professionalism but also trying to emulate it. It was my version of putting on "nice clothes" because guests were coming over; I remained guileless for a long while in terms of stage clothes. What I was actually trying to do was pull off a Mod look from the '60s or '70s—the Jam, the Small Faces, the Who, early Stones—but instead of buying the clothes at cool London vintage stores, I was purchasing them (or stealing them, sometimes) from a shopping mall in Olympia. They were always loose-fitting, saggy-assed, made for an inelegant tomboy. Mostly, I didn't want to be a girl with a guitar. "Girl" felt like an identifier that viewers, especially male ones, saw as a territory upon which an electric guitar was a tourist, an interloper. I wanted the guitar to be an appendage—an extension even—of a body that was made more powerful by my yielding of it.

My look (Mick Jagger in sweatpants?) wasn't trying to make a statement; the premise we all worked from was to be yourself, even if half the time I only knew who I was onstage. It makes for an interesting performance, attempting to both find yourself and lose yourself onstage. That's a lot of pressure on a band, to encompass both menace and protector. But our audience seemed to feel that and need it, too. They found themselves in our songs, saw themselves, felt safe enough to let go only because we'd given them solid ground from which to step off. I'm not being self-aggrandizing—it meant the same to me.

The night before we left Australia, we recorded the ten songs we had written. Laura's roommate Nick Carrol ran cables from the mixing board in his bedroom on the second floor through the hallway, down the stairs, and into the rat-infested, sawdust-covered garage where Corin and I had been both sleeping and rehearsing. With less than fourteen hours until we left the country, we played through the songs live and then tracked our vocals. We did one take, two at the most if we made a mistake we couldn't live with. No overdubs, no redos. Giddy from hearing ourselves on tape and bleary with exhaustion, we sat on the couch while Nick mixed the record until dawn. Then he drove us to the airport and we flew home to America.

Back in Olympia, we remixed the record with Tim Green at the Red House and put it out on Chainsaw Records. It would be self-titled, simple. It was more of a document than an album. A time stamp. We had not quite built the band yet—that would come with our second album—but we had opened the box and pulled out the parts we needed in order to assemble Sleater-Kinney.

CHAPTER 8

CALL THE DOCTOR

Donna Dresch ran Chainsaw Records and was sort of a legend in the Olympia scene: a great guitar player, a shredder with long blond hair and a cool, timeless vibe. She had played with Screaming Trees, the Canadian punks Fifth Column, and Dinosaur Jr., which automatically made her someone you felt was blessing you with her presence. Donna had been to the outer edges of our scene and beyond. But she wasn't a snob; she had a sweet diffidence. She had turned Chainsaw from a zine into a label as a way of putting out her own band, the incendiary Team Dresch, along with other bands she knew and loved. Donna was an out lesbian, had been for as long anyone could remember, and her band got lumped in with an offshoot of punk and indie called queercore. Those identifiers felt important at the time: people were staking out territory, constructing niches in a punk landscape that felt vast. Parceled out like land claims, punk was divided by city, by sound, and by indexers like gender and sexual orientation. But really Team Dresch was a rock band, and a superb one. They stood out for their chops and their fondness for solos and big choruses, all the conventional things that a lot of the punk bands weren't really doing, at least not in Olympia. Team Dresch tore up the stage, allowing their listeners—who included a lot of young queer kids—to act out their audience fantasies in a way they maybe hadn't been allowed to do, or felt safe enough to do, at other shows. As much as the person onstage is performing, so, too, is the audience.

Many of us looked up to Team Dresch, Corin and I included. They were a few years older; they had a lot of experience touring, recording, and putting out records. There was a real intention behind what they were doing, and the music came first. Plus, they were funny—one day they showed up at my and Corin's apartment with a bag of sex toys they'd purchased in Seattle and demoed them in our living room, much to our embarrassment and amusement. They didn't take themselves too seriously even though the stakes were high and their songs were heartfelt. We saw a lot of elements cohere in Team Dresch that we admired. They were bold yet accessible. You could listen to their songs as a guide to surviving, or you could just rock out.

Our drummer, Laura, flew over from Australia in the summer of 1995, and we set up shows along the West Coast. Our first show was on NE Alberta Street in Portland. Now known as the Alberta Arts District—littered with coffee shops, fancy dog boutiques, tea emporiums, and shops selling ice cream apparently worth waiting in line for— at the time it was mostly a Latino and African-American neighborhood with a handful of long-established businesses. Early in the stages of what is a typical gentrification pattern, white and/or punk queers and artists had started moving there for the cheap rent. We played a newly opened lesbian-owned café called Chez What? In the audience were Donna, Kathleen Hanna, Miranda July, our friends and people we looked up to. We played the songs off our first record with the aid—or perhaps hindrance—of a crappy, inadequate vocal PA. No soundcheck. Corin yowled over the drums and the amps we borrowed from the headliner, but my voice couldn't rise above the cacophony. I had no sense of who or what we were as a band; we didn't feel important, more that we had announced our arrival, that we were knocking on the door. Still, I had to concentrate to play and to feel comfortable. People bobbed their heads along to the music. We felt supported, nurtured, but unremarkable. Next we played a club called Moe's in Seattle to about four people, which is such a small crowd that it's hard to tell if you even need to play at all. It's also one more person in the audience than is onstage. The formality, the mystery, any heightened sense of performance is sucked out of the room. But we ran through our songs anyway, smiling awkwardly in between, an awareness forming of the disparity between the sound of our music and what felt like our small, unassuming selves.

We borrowed Corin's father's VW bus for the tour through California, shoving drums and guitars and cables into drawers and cabinets otherwise designed for dishware and camping gear. There was no air conditioning—we misted ourselves with spray bottles of water—and we often had to stop on account of the engine overheating. That summer there were a series of Riot Grrrl "festivals" and "conventions," which were mostly single shows featuring more than four bands and maybe a few people selling fanzines. One of the best aspects of Riot Grrrl was that anyone could adopt the term as their own—it wasn't prescriptive. However, this ambiguity left room for a lot of interpretation. It was on this tour that I witnessed a girl with a tampon as a hair accessory and another with the word "Hippo" written across her T-shirt with a Sharpie. Reclamation had no bounds.

Chainsaw had put out a compilation record and booklet called *Free to Fight*, marrying punk and self-defense. We played some of these shows as well. Team Dresch were at the center of *Free to Fight*, but they brought along instructors, too, creating a combination of musical theater, martial arts, university lecture, and rock show. No mixing of elements felt too conspicuous or incongruous; it was akin to a circus sideshow that was finally getting center stage, even if we were building that stage on our own, a few hours before the show began.

We asked Donna if she would put out our next record. Laura was heading back to Australia, so we needed to set up something quickly before she left. We managed to book a session with John Goodmanson, whom we had each worked with in Heavens to Betsy and Excuse 17, and who had recorded the Bikini Kill and Team Dresch albums. There was a sense of inevitability to everything back then; it all was funneled through the same people, recording- or label-wise, an organism we all fed into.

We recorded *Call the Doctor* in five days.

John and Stu's Recording was housed in a narrow wedge-shaped building on the edge of the Fremont neighborhood in Seattle. Nirvana had recorded *Bleach* there when it was Jack Endino's place, Reciprocal. The small live room had high ceilings, carpet, dartboards and novelty record sleeves on the walls, and an old record player. The control room was tiny. There was no lounge area—you were either in the studio or you were outside, a claustrophobic and immersive experience.

We set up our amps and drums in the main room with no separation save for baffling. We didn't think to adjust sounds or levels between songs or to switch out guitars for a different tone—we just played the songs through until we felt like we'd gotten a good take. We didn't know any other way of recording. We had never worked with a producer before, and John was still coming into his own as one. He was a fantastic engineer, fastidious and fast, capable of harnessing energy and getting good sounds on the fly. He was like a documentarian at the time, present more to observe, capture, and facilitate than to change what we had or who we were. There was really nothing to contemplate anyhow: the recording was perfunctory, the songs were the songs, the sound was the sound, there was nothing to unearth or reveal through the magic of recording. We put some of our vocals through an amp to make them distorted. We doubled guitars on the choruses. John panned Corin's guitar to one side and mine to the other. (If you listen to the album through a busted speaker or headphone, you can only hear half the song.) The whole thing felt as urgent as the title. What more was there to do?

Despite the no-frills approach to recording, the songwriting on *Call the Doctor* brought in characteristics that came to define our sound. On the title track, Corin and I each sang a melody on the chorus. She was louder than me, so her vocal was the lead by default, but we never really considered one a background part to the other. It was a conversation we were having: she had her perspective and I had mine. Or I was emphasizing her point, retelling it even as I was singing along with her. And our guitars did the same thing, augmenting and counteracting each other. We would get to the chorus, and intuitively you'd think this is the time for us to all sing together, that there should be a cohesion, but instead we would split apart. It was almost an anti-chorus. We weren't trying to form a solidarity with anyone but ourselves. Could you sing along to Sleater-Kinney? Sometimes. But we'd just as likely shout over you. And good luck trying to sing along with Corin. Trust me, I know. It's nearly impossible. As a listener you have to decide what to follow in the song, which vocal, which guitar.

This way of writing and of singing was something we tacitly understood. We never discussed it; we never mentioned countermelodies. We didn't want to sing harmonies. Our songs weren't pretty, nor was our style of singing. It sounded scarier to not sing together, rarely allowing the listener to settle into the music. Everything inside the songs was constantly on the verge of breaking apart—Corin's voice, the narrative, the guitars, so few moments provided any respite at all. If we did sing together on the chorus, it was only after a strange, uncomfortable verse. Yet the result was forceful; it sounded like a tightly bound entity, fragments clinging to each other for dear life—if you pulled one thing apart, it wouldn't even sound like a real song. It was a junkyard come to life.

Corin was working at Kit's Camera in the Olympia mall, and many of the songs on *Call the Doctor* address feeling objectified, being watched, as if you're living your life for yourself but with the awareness that it's not just for you, there are other people taking notice, observing. It's a disorienting duality and a tiring scrutiny. So much of working customer service is about self-erasure, subjugating and then selling yourself in order to sell the product, merging with the commodities until you feel like one. Like many young women, we felt like we were on display. Lyrically, the songs read like someone setting off an alarm, trying to transform victimization into power. These are not subtle songs: "They want to socialize you, they want to purify you / They want to dignify and analyze and terrorize you," Corin sings on the title song, followed by "All your life is written for you." Then on "I'm Not Waiting," Corin takes on the role of a voyeur: "Go out on the lawn, put your swimsuit on," she snarls before she reverts to the role of a young girl and sings, "I'm not waiting till I grow up to be a woman." It's an audacious cry, desperately trying for womanhood to be an act of self-possession as opposed to an invitation. But the idea of not waiting until one grows up implies that there is hardly any age that is too young for a woman to be sexualized. "Your words are sticky, stupid, running down my leg." The song has a foreboding creepiness, as if the male gaze and the language that augments it carry an implicit objectification; the power and hurt of words and images are indistinct from the tactile.

For "I Wanna Be Your Joey Ramone," I had driven over to the practice space by myself and written the verses, the guitar part, and the vocal melody. As I often did, I left the chorus open for Corin to sing. "Joey" was really the first song that set a precedent for what would become our habit of meta-songwriting, where we were in a band writing about being in a band, singing about singing. I feel the need to point out that our intent was different from those classic rock songs about being on tour. This isn't us singing about roadies, drugs, and groupies, about watching movies on the bus, about ramblin' on and "takin' care of business." We were in dialogue with ourselves; we responded to and addressed the fans, the critics, and even our own work. Later songs such as "Male Model" or "#1 Must Have" explained the earlier ones ("I Wanna Be Your Joey Ramone," "Little Babies"), discussing what we had already done and why we had done it. There was a sense of substantiation, of clarification.

Joey Ramone was a performer who embodied both gawkiness and grandiosity. He was simultaneously awkward, with his spindly legs and his hair falling into his face, and larger than life. This contradiction seemed to be an ideal metaphor for my own relationship to performing and music: part of me wanted to own the stage, while the other part of me remained uncomfortable with such power.

I suppose some people are born with the certainty that they own sound or volume; that the lexicon of rock music is theirs to borrow from, to employ, to interpret. For them, it might be nothing to move around onstage, to swagger, to sing in front of people, to pick up a guitar, to make records. I set out from a place where I never assumed that those were acceptable choices or that I could be anything but an accessory to rock 'n' roll. The archetypes, the stage moves, the representations of rebellion and debauchery were all male. When Sleater-Kinney first began, it seemed to me that the only way to get a sense of rock 'n' roll was to experience it vicariously. The song was about stepping into someone else's shoes as a means of exploring both my fears and aspirations. I wanted a glimpse of the absurdity, the privilege, and the decadence that hadn't been inherently afforded to us. "I Wanna Be Your Joey Ramone" was a test for ourselves, to see what it felt like to give yourself the smallest amount of power, and to put that power on display, to be unafraid and unafraid of yourself. So in Sleater-Kinney, we sang a lot about a world that we wished we could access without the added explanation or justification. We sang about playing and performing, as if in singing about it, we could really live it, free of judgment or the feeling that we were interlopers. We would project ourselves into a song where we couldn't be impeached. We were stating our validity for the record over and over again, staking our claim, then having to explain it, then drawing yet another line in the sand. In our songs about music, we created our own, new, malleable versions of us, ones that our earnest, overly explanatory selves could pretend to inhabit. Because we felt like outsiders—both in Olympia and Portland, to some extent, but also at festivals and in the mainstream world—we often wrote *about* rock music. We wrote and played ourselves right into existence.

Even with subsequent records, "Joey" was always a reminder not to take what we had for granted, not to create from a place of smugness or entitlement. We were confident, for sure, but we were aware of how uncertainty fomented a sense of having to prove oneself, how it fostered an urgency.

This is where we were starting to grapple with something we would grapple with for the rest of our time as a band: that there was always a sense we were going to have to defend and analyze what we were doing. Why are you in an all-female band? Why do you not have a bass player?

What does it feel like to be a woman in a band? I realized that those questions—that talking about the experience—had become part of the experience itself. More than anything, I feel that this meta-discourse, talking about the talk, is part of how it feels to be a "woman in music" (or a "woman in anything," for that matter—politics, business, comedy, power). There is the music itself, and then there is the ongoing dialogue about how it feels. The two seem to be intertwined and also inescapable. To this day, because I know no other way of being or feeling, I don't know what it's like to be a woman in a band—I have nothing else to compare it to. But I will say that I doubt in the history of rock journalism and writing any man has been asked, "Why are you in an all-male band?"

On the last day of mixing *Call the Doctor*, Corin and I lay on the floor and listened while John played the album back in its entirety. I remembered thinking that we had made a decent record, that I hadn't heard anything that sounded like this before. I don't think I ever really felt that way again about one of our records, simply able to enjoy it without any hyper- or self-criticism. *Call the Doctor* is not our best record, but it was the last one written before any sense of external identity or pressure. When I heard it back, it felt like anthems we'd written for ourselves.

Right after we recorded *Call the Doctor*, we asked Laura to leave the band. The logistics of her living in Australia seemed insurmountable, and there were tensions as well. As a hypochondriac, I was having difficulty with the fact that she was crashing in our apartment. More important, Laura was a songwriter and bandleader at heart, and a talented one. We sensed she wouldn't want to be behind the drums for long, but we had no interest in changing the dynamic of the band. Naturally, Laura was upset, so in the spirit of kindness and open dialogue, a mutual friend of ours suggested that we have a mediated conversation in order to air our grievances. This talk was mediated not by a professional but by a dyed-black-haired metal music fan named Stacey D/C. Suffice it to say, despite our best intentions, there were still a lot of hurt feelings. In hindsight, perhaps we should have paid for a legitimate interlocutor. Dirty deeds done dirt cheap.

During this time I broke up with Corin. We were on a hike at Mount Rainier. It was a sunny day and the views were exquisite, but we were both crying. I spent most of the time staring at my feet and the path. After we talked, we were trapped in this new reality of separateness. The outdoors felt like the smallest room, tight and stifling. We still had to make the long walk to the car and then drive another few hours back to Olympia. I didn't know how to be so entwined with someone: in a band, in a relationship, in the same apartment. Selfishly, naively, I wanted nothing to change. I wanted to still be close to Corin, for there to be continued trust and joy and for the music to be an extension of those very things. In reality, it would be much more brutal and heartbreaking.

We toured for *Call the Doctor* with Toni Gogin on drums. Toni was a Portland punk kid, soft-spoken, with short, spiky hair, a sensitive tomboy. She played guitar and drummed a little and we had toured with her other group, the CeBe Barnes Band. We booked the tour ourselves. We'd go over to K Records (whose capacious headquarters doubled as a reference library) and someone would hand over a list of addresses and phone numbers, with contact names if we were lucky. Not everything on the list was current, especially in less-visited cities like Fargo or Lincoln—some venues were already closed by the time you called, likely only open for a few months, just a VFW hall or warehouse where some kids put on shows for a summer. For the most part, and especially when trying to set up all-ages shows, you were dealing with someone your own age, a student who booked events at their college, young people who were running a space. We rarely played bars or 21+ shows. We were getting paid around $350 per show at most, and that was for the college shows where they'd cut you an actual check. We played Yale to four or five people. The campus is walled off, so we literally stood outside the gates ringing a bell to get in. We felt like the hired help. Toni slept in the van that night and got booted off the lot by security.

We scraped by on merch money. ("Merch" is short for "merchandise": T-shirts, records, posters, hoodies, hats. And in the case of really savvy artists: dog sweaters, bibs, keychains, laser pointers, and limited-edition coffee.) Donna and Chainsaw had underestimated how many albums we'd sell, so our record was sold out just about everywhere. We couldn't afford hotels—we were sleeping on floors in strangers' houses, and on long drives we'd catch up on sleep in the van. In the back of our vehicle we had built a loft with a dual purpose. One was to create a lockbox of sorts for the gear, so that if someone broke into the front of the van, they couldn't get to the musical equipment. But the storage space didn't go all the way to the ceiling, so on top was a precarious perch of sorts where one of us could sleep. It was extremely dangerous, speeding down the highway, one of us loose in the loft, inches from the roof, on a dusty foam mattress covered in a sheet we never bothered to wash, mixed in with extra luggage, T-shirts boxes, and stray used Kleenexes.

Tour is a strange beast. What constitutes comfort and cleanliness is relative. In 1996, I was twenty-two. I slept on couches that had been purchased at Goodwill or hauled in from the sidewalk. I made a bed on

In an Olympia alleyway. Getting ready to leave on the Heavens to Betsy and Excuse 17 tour with (left to right) *Corin, CJ Phillips, Tracy Sawyer, and Becca Albee.*

any number of surfaces with unknown, unsavory provenances. I showered in plastic stalls mottled with mold, and borrowed shampoo, toothpaste, and even towels. I never wore slippers. At night, we'd haul in the foam mattress from the van, which we had nicknamed "P.M." for "pube magnet," since all it did was collect small stray hairs that would be carted back to the van and stick with us for the remainder of tour. From the stage we'd politely ask for a place to stay, a humbling process that negates any sense of coolness or respectability.

On U.S. tours I would read novels about the states through which we were passing, trying to populate the vastness—the long stretches of green and brown and grays—with characters I could grow to know and love. Willa Cather kept me company in Nebraska and the upper Midwest. I read Joseph Mitchell essays about the Bowery and tales from James Baldwin's Harlem before arriving in New York. Capote's *Other*

Voices, Other Rooms accompanied me through the South. For the West Coast I brought along Joan Didion essays and the writing of Wallace Stegner. Books grounded me, helped me to feel less alone. Technically I was around people all the time on tour, but I often felt estranged from my bandmates, unknown. Perhaps this was depression, a murkiness that distorted and disabled connection. I drifted in and out of this darkness, pulled away, then reappeared.

In Atlanta, after playing a show during which a gaggle of topless women took over the stage during our set, we ended up at a house owned by a gregarious rockabilly dyke named Rizzo. She must have stayed at her girlfriend's that night because we let ourselves into her house. Inside were two pit bulls, one of which was in heat, bloody towels on the kitchen floor. I slept under a leather S&M-clad mannequin hung from the ceiling in the bedroom.

Another option was to crash at the promoter's house or with the opening band. I rested my weary head on unwashed pillows in beds we were lucky enough to get because someone's roommate was out of town. We slept in dorm room bunk beds after college shows or on industrial sofas in the common areas of university housing. But mostly we slept on floors, rolling out sleeping bags a few inches from one another, no privacy, no distinction between one grimy human shape and another, stinky breath and feet and snores and twitches all merging into a feral pile; it was an endless, slovenly slumber party.

Tour is the aspect of being in a band that many people assume is the most glamorous. Perhaps you imagine a private jet filled with champagne and puppies, backstage areas with white leather couches and ornate lamps, an on-call barista, a masseuse. And, yes, all this *is* possible, but it will cost you. Though I know of bands that travel with exercise machines, personal chefs, fitness trainers, and Persian rugs, most musicians—even ones headlining major festivals and selling out large-scale shows—have a goal of making tour profitable. They'd rather spend money on production and design, on bringing extra musicians, on lighting and sound rigs rather than, say, a chocolate waterfall in their dressing room.

During the early years of touring I came to the realization that we were just as much movers as we were musicians. After all, without the benefit of a crew, essentially what we did each night was pack and unpack, load and unload, and lift heavy objects from vans into rooms and then back into vans. The plainness of those actions, the bluntness, is so much of what I remember about *Call the Doctor*. The album took what is rote and routine and made the motions desperate, alluring, a trap. We blamed the simplification of our identities and the outside world's doubt in our abilities not only on sexism but on a paucity of imagination. We were monsters, we weren't like you. We might have been movers but we were coming to steal what you thought was yours.

CHAPTER 9

MEDIATED

Even though we were playing tiny shows, tumbling across the country in a petri dish of a van, *Call the Doctor* was attracting the attention of both audiences and critics. Robert Christgau came to our sparsely attended Bryn Mawr show to interview us for a feature in the *Village Voice*. I stood next to him in the back of the room while the opening band played, discussing college and what I was studying (sociolinguistics), trying to impress him more with my intelligence than with requisite rock slickness or aloofness, neither of which I possessed.

We took the photos for the *Voice* in the venue bathroom, Corin, Toni, and I pressed up against one another in a side hug, ragtag and babyfaced, in thrift-store coats, with uneven dye jobs and gelled, unwashed hair. We didn't know how to pose except like in photobooth strips, or like pictures we'd seen in magazines or books. We tried out various looks—angry! coy! confused! Sometimes I think the best you can ever feel in a photo shoot is like a sexy clown. We were more in the cute vein—or just weird—huddled together in the early confusion and excitement of it all. It was 1996.

Then Corin and Toni and I did a photo shoot for *Spin*, where I wore the same outfit as I had for the *Village Voice*. At the time, *Spin* was the biggest national publication to cover our band. Clad in a red coat from Goodwill, my hair dyed black, cut shorter in the back and angling down toward my face in a steep slope, and Corin doe-eyed in faux fur, we did our best to look like a real rock band. In other words, we pouted and pointed. It was fun, goofy, and very unrefined. My excitement for the eventual release of the article was palpable. I was eager to exist in a familiar and known context where my pursuits might be validated, not so much by the public—though that was part of it—but by my parents and grandparents. Anything that might help rationalize my not attending graduate school or my clear lack of a "backup plan."

So I was full of hopefulness and anticipation when my father called a few weeks later to tell me that he had seen the magazine. I had yet to see the issue. The first thing I asked about was the photo. Did I look okay? Yes, he said, the photo is fine. Then there was a pause. He asked if there was something I wanted to tell him. He sounded stifled and awkward. I said no, confused by this line of questioning. My father then told me that the *Spin* article stated that Corin and I had dated.

Neither Corin nor I had ever told the journalist that piece of information, nor was it something we had ever mentioned to our parents or anyone in our families.

I felt like the ground had been pulled out from underneath me. My stomach dropped. I lay on my bed. I told my dad that Corin and I *had* dated but that we didn't anymore, which was the truth. I said that I didn't think or know if I was gay, dating Corin was just something that had happened, which at the age of twenty-two was also the truth. It was a conversation that sounded like Morse code. A string of words. Pause. More words. Pause. Waiting. Waiting for some kind of resolution. Finally my dad said that he was cool with it. (This was almost two

Around age three, with a Kool-Aid hat and matching jacket.
Luther Burbank Park, Washington.

My first professional photo shoot, ostensibly for that year's holiday card.

On account of my father's job, we had a lot of Peterbilt Trucks paraphernalia. Also, this is the first documentation of a lifelong love of mine: plaid and checkered shirts.

The Brownstein family: my mother, father, and sister.
Outside our home in Bellevue, Washington.

A high school camping trip to the Washington coast. 1992.

With Corin on the California coast during a day off from the *Call the Doctor* tour.

Sleater-Kinney doing a group vocal take in 2000 during the recording of *All Hands on the Bad One*.

Driving back to Olympia from the SeaTac airport with a copy of the first magazine in which Sleater-Kinney was featured.

Our first ever Sleater-Kinney show. Sydney, Australia.
With Stephen O'Neil from the Cannanes on drums.

At John and Stu's during the
recording of *Dig Me Out*.

Ballarat, Australia. Playing our drummer
Laura MacFarlane's guitar.

Soundcheck at Madison Square Garden on our tour with Pearl Jam.

Polaroid outtake from the front cover shoot for *Dig Me Out*.

ABOVE: Polaroid outtake from a *Magnet* magazine cover shoot.

LEFT: A classic example of my "business casual" stage attire.

A concert for Food Not Bombs at Dolores Park in San Francisco. Opening for Fugazi.

A picture of every single person who watched our set at a festival in Dour, Belgium.

With Corin Tucker, Tracy Sawyer, and Becca Albee on the joint Heavens to Betsy and Excuse 17 tour. Affixed to the back of the passenger seat is a sign Excuse 17 had to put up explaining and apologizing for the fact that we had a boy drummer at a "Girls Only" show.

Photo by John Clark

Showing off my first tattoo in Janet's backyard on SE Market Street in Portland. From the *One Beat* cover shoot.

So serious. Touring for *The Hot Rock* in Japan.

years before my father would come out to me.) "Cool with it"—it was a strange phrase. Reassuring, yes, but benign. Like so many things, it just felt like another part of my world that didn't have an architecture or a name.

Then I called Corin. Her parents had also seen the article. Her mom said it made her feel sick.

When I finally saw the issue of *Spin* for myself, it was the first time I felt like I was reading about someone I didn't know. The writer characterized me as a burbling groupie of Corin's, casting me as obsequious and frivolous. I wasn't reading about myself; I was reading about a character the writer had made up to fit his tendentious point of view about the band, a narrative he was creating that we needed to fit inside.

There is the identity you have in a band or as an artist when you exist for no one other than yourself, or for your co-conspirators, your co-collaborators. When you own the sounds and when who you are is whoever you want to be. There are no definitions as prescribed by outsiders, strangers; you feel capricious, full of contradictions, and areas of yourself feel frayed or blurred. Other times you feel resolute or whole. But it's all a part of you, it doesn't feel fractured, just mutable. But once your sound exits that room, it is no longer just yours—it belongs to everyone who hears it. And who you are is at the mercy of the audience's opinions and imagination. If you haven't spent any time deliberately and intentionally shaping your narrative, if you're unprepared, like I was, then one will be written for you. And if you already feel like a fractured self, you will start to feel like a broken one.

That's how I felt the day I was outed: splintered and smashed. I had not yet figured out who I was, and now I was robbed of the opportunity to publicly do so, to be in flux. Though the writer had gotten it wrong, I also think there was no way he could have gotten it right. My external persona was open and mercurial, and internally I was something far more complex, at least more multifaceted than a profile could capture or that I wanted to share. From that point on, any denial or rescinding would seem like backpedaling or shame to a group of people whom I didn't want to alienate. Yet I felt it was unfair to be labeled when I had yet to find a label for myself, and when binary, fixed identities held no meaning or safety for me.

Thus, I decided to retreat, to put the energy further into the performance. My persona would not be about artifice or flamboyancy, it would not be alien or otherworldly, it would be about kineticism, it would be about movement. Again I returned to the notion that my salvation was to be in motion. I would be galvanic onstage, so that offstage I could try to figure out how to eventually live with a stillness, with myself.

CHAPTER 10

HELLO, JANET

I'm not above superstition. Ask me about how not being on page 13 of a book or magazine—or on any page numbers that add up to 13—when a plane is taking off keeps it from crashing. Or how touching both sides of the aircraft as I board, petting it as one would a golden retriever, keeps it aloft. It's how I've flown safely for decades. Well, that and the guitar pick I keep in my back pocket and the talisman my friend gave me that belonged to her father. I'm practically a copilot.

One day I was carrying a full-length mirror in Toni's basement (rehearsing in domestic spaces often requires negotiations with and the transference of household goods). As I rounded a corner, the mirror slipped from my hands and broke. I knew this event was supposed to signify seven years of bad luck. Yet somehow I sensed the mirror breaking meant that Sleater-Kinney was the opposite of cursed; it felt more like a conjuring, of serendipity and fortune, some outside force that would take us. It was also a sign.

There's a long drumroll in "Call the Doctor" where the song builds to a crescendo that then breaks open in cathartic release. Toni nailed nearly every change in the songs, but she could not for the life of her tame this roll. Every night on tour she would mess it up, going into the next section either early or late. Corin couldn't lock in with her to form anything resembling a rhythm section. This drumroll got in Toni's head to the point that it became impossible for her to succeed. It was a crucial moment, and we couldn't count on her; it felt deflating and anti-climactic every time. One night on tour, pushed to the point of frustration and embarrassment, I turned around and yelled, "Fuck you!" after she botched the part. It is a moment of which I am not proud. Corin and I were exasperated and began to worry that we wouldn't get to the next place with Toni. We had to fire her.

Shortly after, *Interview* magazine got in touch. They were doing a requisite "women in music" feature for their November 1996 issue, and they wanted to include me along with Team Dresch's Donna and Jody. I ended up in a pair of baggy designer trousers four sizes too big, a ribbed turtleneck, and my own coat, since it was the only outer layer that fit. Jody wore a blazer and no shirt, putting duct tape on her nipples, part protest, part lack of a better option. Donna wore a men's suit. It was shoddy and unsophisticated. We looked like thrift-store couches covered up with clean, ill-fitting sheets in preparation for a parental visit, hiding the stains and lumpy cushions. Since it was the fanciest shoot any of us had done—complete with the photographer blasting music in the stark white studio—we tried our very best. The makeup artist that day was named Marnie, and when I mentioned to her that Sleater-Kinney was currently short a band member, she told me she knew of a drummer I might want to check out. Her name was Janet Weiss.

Corin had moved from Olympia to Portland after she'd graduated college and after our breakup. Now she was living off Alder Street in the southeast part of the city along with Jody and a woman named Anna. Anna owned a rescued Rottie mix, Puppa, who was one of those dogs that comes with a set of instructions when you walk in the door: "Don't make eye contact," "She doesn't like hats," "Never play late-period Led Zeppelin in her presence." Rumor had it that at her previous residence, all the roommates had gathered for a human/dog/professional trainer therapy session. We had to carefully sidestep her to make it to the basement stairs.

There could be an entire coffee-table book (and maybe there is) devoted to basement practice spaces. If you don't grow up in a large, apartment-based city, then your first rehearsal space was likely a garage or basement. Attempts at giving these rooms any vibe at all can be difficult, especially when you're pushing aside your dad's lawn mower to make room for the amps. Even when you're living in your own house in your early twenties—sharing it with five or eight people—creating a room that is suitable for music is not an easy task. But sure, nail a few cots to the wall for soundproofing, cover it with concert flyers, and plug in a lamp. It's shabby chic meets fire hazard. A busted staircase without a railing was optional, but not required. A dead possum rotting in the walls? Sure. The basement practice space at Corin's resembled a mineshaft. It was a half-finished room, part foundation, part dirt, replete with a bright, unforgiving bare bulb.

Janet arrived at Corin's front door one afternoon with shiny black pigtails and a snare drum. She was nine years older than me and part of the more vintage-y Portland set at the time, the "Cocktail Nation" that exalted vintage dresses for the girls and suits and skinny ties for the boys. It was a clean-cut aesthetic, part Mod, part moped, with just a hint of louinginess mixed in. They were stylish and adult—at least it felt like that to me. I was not yet twenty-three. And though I had traveled around the country and halfway across the world I still hadn't found a way out of my college town.

The three of us slunk past Puppa and went down to the basement. Corin and I had some new songs we'd been playing on a West Coast tour with Toni, but only one stood out, and it felt like a good one with which to audition Janet. The song was built around my guitar riff: fast and careening, a skid into a crash, then it reset. Corin's vocals were desperate and angry—even in the relatively quiet bits there was a viciousness. The melody was a frantic headshake, though whether it was a "no" or a "yes," I wasn't sure; it was past that, on the brink of oblivion, frenzied yet resolute. The tune was an outsized, fevered version of her, of me, of us. We called it "Dig Me Out."

Janet hit the drums harder than anyone we'd played with. Corin and I were used to having drummers follow along and defer to us; they were percussive cheerleaders or meandering, interpretive artists, serving as more of an augmentation than an equal component. Immediately Janet grounded the song in a way we'd never heard, giving each of our guitar parts a place to go. Janet had learned all the songs from *Call the Doctor* as well. She bashed out a body, a spine, finally making that album title sound like an order and not a plea.

So now we had a drummer, but it was still on a trial basis. We had already been through four—Misty Farrell (who played on the first 7-inch single), Stephen, Laura, and Toni—and we wanted someone permanent, a collaborator. Janet would join us for the CMJ Music Marathon in New York, after which we loosely and mutually agreed that we would decide whether to make it official or not.

CMJ—which stands for *College Media Journal*, though the magazine was long ago renamed *CMJ New Music Monthly*—is a music industry trade show that takes place in New York every fall. The showcases, pre–digital age, felt not unlike an auction, or a high school talent show writ large. They did what the Internet and social media do now on a daily basis, which is to highlight and amplify certain acts. The main difference is that CMJ took place in a physical space (or spaces) where you gathered once a year, and in a matter of days tried to make sense of who was the most exciting band, which musician had the most hype, who utterly surprised or thoroughly disappointed, and who would get signed. Back then, CMJ was attended mostly by labels, journalists, music publishers, and booking agents. It was very much an industry showcase at which unsigned artists could find representation and where everyone was vying to be deemed the "next big thing."

College radio and what CMJ stood for was actually quite viable in the '80s and '90s. Now CMJ is known mostly as an acronym, but there was a time when it was both part of a serious strategic goal and also a market unto itself. Particularly for independent bands and musicians, charting on college radio or having a local DJ promoting your music was extremely important; it could affect album and tour sales and was nearly as important as having a label. So established was this subsidiary market—along with who it championed and what artists had success within it—that it came to identify a genre in and of itself. Sleater-Kinney arrived at the tail end of a time when "college rock" bands were in fact a thing.

The trip out east with Janet was whirlwind, four shows in four days. Our official CMJ showcase was at a club called the Cooler in the meatpacking district, playing with a handful of bands associated with the Pacific Northwest like Unwound and Modest Mouse. A long and eager line snaked around the block and the crowd continued to pour in until the numbers far exceeded a safe capacity. The show was oversold by a grossly negligent and dangerous amount, an absolute fire hazard. I recall little of playing other than feeling a drenched, dizzying excitement. The walls of the venue literally dripped with perspiration—they were glistening with sweat, just shy of tropical.

We also packed onto even smaller stages, such as Coney Island High and the lesbian bar Meow Mix. Mike D from the Beastie Boys was at the latter venue, along with Sonic Youth's Thurston Moore. Even though we'd meant it respectfully and playfully, I hoped Thurston wasn't mad that we'd referenced him in our "Joey Ramone" song. It was thrilling and nerve-racking alike; people we looked up to were starting to take notice. I was too shy at the time, however, to say much of anything to those musicians as they stood in line.

That night on the sidewalk outside Meow Mix, a young guy with wavy hair and a warm, easy smile approached us. He was with the singer/songwriter Lois Maffeo, whom we knew from Olympia. He told us he loved our music and he lingered around awhile to chat. A few months later a package arrived for us at Kill Rock Stars. In it were two black VHS cases with silver writing on them, fastidiously neat and in all caps. They were addressed to Corin and me. Corin's case featured a long note, explaining how her music had changed his life. The words were sweet and sentimental, poetic and charming. Mine simply said "Carrie." The tapes were from Lance Bangs. Three years later he and Corin were married.

Those first Sleater-Kinney shows with Janet felt wild, fervent. We had seldom put much thought into performance, sound quality, or equipment. The plan was always simple, maybe even feral: play, emote. Start the song, then stay with the song until you are the song. I didn't think about what I was wearing or put on any makeup. Our music was its own theater, it created a heightened world on its own so we didn't have to. But now hype was building up around our band—we'd been featured in the *Village Voice* and *Spin*, music critic Greil Marcus was writing about us, we'd been incubating, poised. Then all of a sudden we got to New York and it became real.

And in Janet, despite the stress of living up to the accolades, we realized that we had a drummer who was not only good enough but extraordinary. We realized we might be able to succeed in fulfilling expectations, others' and also our own. Our songs and our sound now had an anchor and a backbone that Corin and I could rest upon. We felt a huge sense of relief.

Janet was the best decision we ever made. She was no-nonsense and outgoing, olive-skinned with sleek, jet-black hair and blunt bangs. Her look, like her determination, was signature, unwavering, and ageless. She was the cool one, the social one, and we could count on her to attend after-parties and play pool with the opening bands on our behalf while Corin and I retreated to our hotel rooms early to shower, read, and sleep. Forget drummer jokes, Janet is one of the most musically intelligent people I know. And she was certainly the most musically gifted member of the band, the one with the largest musical lexicon and sphere from which to draw influence and reference. Janet was also the road dog of the band, a term used to describe the lifers, the ones who can live on the road and feel as at home there as they do in their own beds at night. Me, on other hand, I always wanted to magically transport myself back to my own house after each show, a feeling that sometimes left me feeling splintered on tour. While Corin and I shaped the world of Sleater-Kinney from the inside, conspiratorially, as if from a bunker, Janet was able to see the bigger picture, translating the secret handshake into a more universal greeting.

CHAPTER 11

SELLOUTS

With the modest success of *Call the Doctor* and our CMJ buzz, a fair bit of attention had turned toward the band. Chainsaw was the tiniest of indie labels, and we had the inkling to look elsewhere to take the next step. An obvious front-runner was Kill Rock Stars, the Olympia-based label run by Slim Moon, who had put out Bikini Kill and Elliott Smith, among others. They had a diverse roster and the label was a statement as much as anything, the moniker itself like a middle finger aimed at profligate decadence. But there were a slew of other great indie labels across the country, and major labels, too, some who were quite interested in seeing what was next for us.

We met with A&R people from Warner Bros., London, and Geffen. (The A&R—artists and repertoire—division of a label is responsible for scouting and developing talent.) People—men—took us out to gluttonous, exclamatory-laden dinners previously of the sort we'd only experienced for birthdays and graduations. The kind of meal where I felt license to order soda *and* wine, with refills on both. They also paid for us to stay in swank New York City hotels. The Soho Grand had just opened, and we each got our own room for the first time in the band's history. I called my friends from the phone in the room, ordered ice cream sundaes, and stayed in bed the entire time, wanting to relish every second of this novelty excess. We borrowed a convertible Cabriolet from one A&R guy and drove to a show at the Middle East in Boston with what we could fit of our equipment jammed into the trunk. For all the time we'd spent being suspicious of or even vilifying major labels, this courtship had a humanizing effect. Everyone was kind, intelligent, genuinely interested in the band.

While in New York we also met with Matador Records. Home to albums and artists I adored at the time—Liz Phair, Yo La Tengo, Guided by Voices, Pavement, Helium—Matador had more muscle than most of the indies back home in the Pacific Northwest. Matador felt like—and should have been—a viable contender. With label cofounder Gerard Cosloy's keen ear and prescience coupled with the savvy business and social acumen of his partner, Chris Lombardi, Matador was not only capable and successful, it was cool, free of preciousness or folksiness. It had a wide-reaching and solid reputation, a presence. Moreover, it was cosmopolitan, like a relative you might fantasize about growing up to be, who lives in the big city and sends theater and art reviews, teaches you about bourbon and millineries, hip and savvy, brimming with strategy and game. Matador was a legitimate possibility, mostly because they offered us a sense of one. So why didn't we sign to Matador?

My attitude may have been a factor.

Our meeting with Matador was in the early afternoon. I hadn't eaten anything, and I was famished, agitated, and fidgety from low blood sugar. I told Janet and Corin that I'd join them momentarily and I walked into a chain restaurant that sells creamy soups in bread bowls, food that can best be described as pale and needing sun. I sat down and very. slowly. and. deliberately. ate. I savored every bite of the chowder that was coagulating inside the circular loaf. I added saltine crackers and got a refill of soda. I watched the minutes go by, aware of my lateness growing conspicuous, less careless, more insolent. Forty-five minutes after my bandmates had arrived, I walked into the office. I entered with the willingness of a teenager who's been asked to clean her room on a Friday evening. I was sullen, distant. I might as well have been wearing a hooded sweatshirt and sucking my thumb. Any lightness or curiosity I normally possessed was cloaked, clenched, choked. I was a sweaty fist. Janet and Corin glared at me as I joined them at a large conference table, the conversation already in progress.

In contrast to my raincloud freakshow, the employees at Matador were bright, eager, and friendly. They talked us through their plan and the label infrastructure, pitching us on their capabilities and enthusiasm. I only showed momentary interest and a glimpse of levity when, as the meeting concluded, we toured the warehouse. I stocked up on their entire catalog in vinyl.

I was acting out an unfocused haughtiness. I felt out of control. We should have left the meeting victorious and proud, at the very least excited. Instead I felt indignant, contrarian. Janet and Corin were justifiably angry and confounded. With no manager to ameliorate anxieties, to mediate, and to be the voice of reason or tie-breaker, we had only one another. There would be many decisions in Sleater-Kinney dictated not by reason but by fear, working from a place of consensus, like some high-minded, well-meaning nonprofit board, except these were our lives and careers. We fumbled around for a place that felt good, a space often situated right next to someone else feeling awful. It was a delicate balance. We had to go with what felt right, even if the decisions were wrong.

Fortunately, my immaturity didn't win out, at least not immediately. There was a serious discussion to be had, and Matador was part of that.

Many of my reservations about signing to one of these larger labels could be boiled down to—I'll borrow a phrase from an old Cat Power record—"What would the community think?" In 1996, if you lived in Olympia, like I did, or were part of any number of underground music scenes across the United States or even abroad, signing to a major label was resolutely considered "selling out." Ambition itself seemed anathema, or at the very least drew skepticism. To court fame, money, and press felt dirty, sweaty—it implied you wanted to be accepted and loved by the mainstream, the same people who had rejected, taunted, and diminished you in high school. Jocks. Cheerleaders. Preppies. Yuppies. It sounds silly now but at the time these categories seemed finite, immutable, and significant.

Much of it boiled down to identity, a way of differentiating punk from the rest of the world, making it subversive, confrontational. Whether quiet or loud, fast or slow, pretty or ugly—it was not about a sound or look—punk was about making choices that didn't bend to consumptive and consumerist inclinations and ideologies, that didn't commodify the music or ourselves. We didn't want to be associated with a brand. Mostly, we didn't want to *be* a brand. There was no middle ground. We came from a very specific context and it was difficult to imagine existing, let alone succeeding, outside of it.

One assumption in the 1990s went like this: if you dressed a certain way, or were hanging around in any sort of artistic milieu, then you must know a lot about music (not to mention the concomitant film and art movements). I was so accustomed to hanging out with music nerds, and being one myself, that I imagined everyone must love music with the same fervor as me and possess encyclopedic knowledge of it to boot.

We also subscribed to codified aesthetics; they created a shorthand. Part of it was on account of less immediate access to material goods; they were not at one's fingertips and instead required long hours in record or book stores talking to clerks and other customers, rentals of videos, attending obscure film festivals, and doing a copious amount of collecting and borrowing. The seeking was tactile, the process of discovery more arduous but also highly interactive. And that effort really grounded the learning into contexts, chronologies, and histories. Making certain sartorial choices—hair dyed green or shaved on the side, a JFA or Diamanda Galás sticker on a three-ring binder, a book by Genet tucked under an arm, dressing up for school like a character from *Twin Peaks*—these were all signifiers so that we could locate other outsiders quickly. It didn't mean we shared an entirely similar worldview or that we had grown up with the same set of experiences, but it was something, it was a wink and a nod. Nowadays, leather jackets don't predict a love of Marlon Brando or the Ramones any more than skinny jeans indicate an affinity with Johnny Thunders or a striped boatneck shirt and pixie cut affirm that one's a fan of Godard and *Breathless*. With access to everything, we can dabble without really knowing. I am not bemoaning a diminishing awareness of references, but it's easier than ever to be divorced from both provenance and predecessors, to essentially be a cultural tease.

The esoteric and extraneous knowledge of musical minutiae is still embedded deep within me, developed during those formative years as a means of social currency and credibility. Sometimes, I reflexively default to the reactionary and the habitual. For instance, if someone mentions Rites of Spring, I assume they could just as easily be talking about the band from Washington, D.C., as Stravinsky. And once we start discussing D.C. punk, we might as well mention (as to really stress our perspicacity!) lesser-known groups like Ignition, the Warmers, and Circus Lupus. If you say STP, I know that means one of Julie Cafritz's bands post–Pussy Galore, not the Stone Temple Pilots. You want to talk about Kevin Rowland and the early days of Dexy's? The connection between Dolly Mixture and the Damned? Howard Devoto, first with Buzzcocks and then with Magazine? Let's! Tubeway Army? That's Gary Numan, pre-"Cars" and at his most droll. Really, I get you; we have so much in common. The facts are often arcane, but like any memorized code, they mark a kind of inclusion, a competency. And though perhaps it's a lexicon on its way to extinction, I suppose it's still a way of quickly locating a fellow traveler.

Protecting your group and ethos required a rigidity. The tacit agreement you entered into when you became part of an underground or indie music scene was that to go mainstream had the potential to water down—or be an inevitable compromise—of your art. Furthermore, it could put you in conflict with your community, potentially damaging it, certainly operating at the expense or denial of it. The notion of the mainstream's toxicity wasn't always an outright discussion at parties or among friends—again, the rules were implied and entrenched—but abundant treatises about selling out could be found in zines like *Punk Planet* or *Maximum RocknRoll*. By the time Sleater-Kinney was a band, there was very little question that the context from which we came was one of fairly radical politics.

If nothing else, I was living in a town that had once been home to Kurt Cobain. The simplified version of his story could be reduced to a guy who signed to a major label, got so famous that he felt alienated from his audience, and then killed himself. And Nirvana had done it right—they had changed the weather, they had rewritten the rules, their music had mattered. And then: death. This tragedy was now in the figurative guidebook—it functioned as a cautionary tale. To wish for more was to wish for something potentially, crushingly horrible. So if you did wish for more, you had to keep it a secret.

We chose Kill Rock Stars. We stayed close to home.

The thing is, Sleater-Kinney was ambitious. We didn't only want to preach to the choir, to the already-converted. We knew there was a potential audience in parts of the country that didn't have a "scene," an infrastructure. That there were people who wouldn't hear about us via word of mouth or fanzines or independent record stores. Some people might only be exposed to our band if we were featured in larger magazines or sold our albums in big-box stores. Eventually, I started to cringe at the elitism that was often paired with punk and the like. A movement that professed inclusiveness seemed to actually be highly exclusive, as alienating and ungraspable as many of the clubs and institutions that drove us to the fringes in the first place. One set of rules had simply been replaced by new ones, and they were just as difficult to follow.

CHAPTER 12

DIG ME OUT

Half of the album *Dig Me Out* was written in my apartment on South Capitol Way in Olympia. Corin came up from Portland and sublet a room in a nearby house. We sat around on my cheap pleather furniture in a living room with wall-to-wall industrial blue carpet and wrote "Turn It On" and "Little Babies." Lance had come to visit and I felt distraught. Corin was in a new place, falling in love. Still heartbroken by me. I wanted her to stick around, but she was gone.

Though Corin and I had split up, there was never a question we wouldn't stay together as a band. That also never gave us time to process the end of the relationship, except within the songs. Nearly every song on *Dig Me Out* is either about me or Lance—which probably seems obvious to any listener or fan of the band who knows even a modicum of backstory. Even if you didn't, you could listen to a song like "One More Hour" or "Jenny" or "Little Babies" or "Turn It On" and know that these were songs about love and desire, both lost and found. But I didn't know any of the songs were about me. In my ability to compartmentalize and subsume feelings, I blithely focused on the melody, the riffs, anything but what was actually being sung. And if I did tune in, it was with a psychic distance and detachment. Who is "Jenny"? Who is the person with the "darkest eyes" in "One More Hour"? Certainly not me.

"Little Babies" is a song that sounds like it's about the fans, and maybe it is. But later I realized that it was probably also about me, some confluence of Corin's caretaking role toward both me and the audience, feeling taken for granted and misunderstood by both. The role of a woman onstage is often indistinct from her role offstage—pleasing, appeasing, striking some balance between larger-than-life and iconic with approachable, likable, and down-to-earth, the fans like gaping mouths, hungry for more of you.

Being in a band with an ex, and both being songwriters and lyricists, takes a lot of compassion and understanding. Sometimes I think Corin and I fell back into a kind of platonic love by learning about each other through the songs we were writing. Since we sing on each other's songs, and often have to write lyrics that work in conjunction with one another, we were forced to live inside the other person's story, her perspective, her ache. We forgave each other, we empathized with later struggles, loss, and heartbreak, we witnessed growth and progress and change. We found each other again in the music, eventually.

Recently I asked Corin what she meant by "Don't say another word about the other girl" in the break of "One More Hour." There had never been anyone else and she knew that. At first she couldn't even recall if it was about someone in particular, a specific jealousy. Finally she said it was about all the people she thought wanted me, which, as I thought about my twenty-two-year-old cherubic self with a terrible dye job, sounded silly, and we both laughed. These are the moments I cherish with Corin, that we can shine a shared fondness on our past, like we have the same flashlight. There are no longer any dark corners.

Sleater-Kinney recorded *Dig Me Out* over ten days in the winter of

1996. With a tiny budget that didn't include housing, the three of us stayed with my father at my childhood home in Redmond. John and Stu's studio didn't have heat, so we set up a series of radiant space heaters. We played in sweaters and coats and did dance aerobics routines both to amuse ourselves and to stay warm. We did a few keyboard and guitar overdubs but we basically tracked live save for the vocals. As on *Call the Doctor*, John panned one of the guitars to the left and the other to the right. And, again, we didn't switch guitar settings or amps in between songs.

Halfway through the recording, it snowed heavily enough that we were unable to make it back across the 520 bridge to Redmond. We were too broke to get a hotel room, so I asked my mother and her husband if we could crash at their house in Seattle. I was twenty-two and had never once stayed with my mother after she moved out. I had never spent a night in one of the apartments she lived in, not once. My mother's house was in the Montlake neighborhood. Designed by her husband, Eric, a civil engineer, the house was steely inside and out, concrete, gray on gray, like some beached cubist whale. He had built it prior to marrying or even meeting my mother, which is why I always found the double shower in the master bedroom so off-putting, but I suppose a less cynical side of myself would call it optimistic.

Entering my mother's world in the middle of recording was disorienting. Since leaving our family, she and I had been in sporadic and often tumultuous contact, seeing each other maybe only once a year. I was still quite hurt and angry. When we did visit each other, I couldn't help but try to gauge her health, her weight. Was she substantial enough to carry anything around other than her own needs? She looked healthier now, happier. Nevertheless, she and Eric felt like a childless couple we were visiting, even though I was technically her child. The couches were covered in plastic to avoid the cats scratching them, and there was very little in the way of knickknacks or niceties. It felt like a W hotel lobby with Joan Osborne and Patty Griffin playing instead of electronic music. They made us cookies and called each other "baby" and "boo boo." To this day I can't tell you who is who, though I imagine they are both baby *and* boo boo.

Corin and Janet and I settled in for two nights. With no official guest room in the house, we slept on the living room floor in sleeping bags or under blankets. We speculated about album artwork. We watched *Pop Up Video* on VH1 and played cards. We talked about calling the record *Dig Me Out*, at this point not just for the title of the song but because we were literally stuck in the snow, trapped at my mother's house, unable to go into the studio, our van immobilized at the bottom of a hill. Those nights with Janet and Corin, it felt like being in the band had become its own version of family. They were there to insulate me against the craziness I felt by being in this strange house. On the second morning, when cabin fever had set in and my mother had clearly reached the end of her hostessing threshold (one night, it turned out), we walked to the van and shoveled it out from the snow. Janet got in the driver's seat and did the requisite forward/backward technique to wrest the vehicle from its frosty hold. A softball-size chunk of ice flew from the back tire, missing Corin and me by a few inches, and smashed a window of the car behind us. We left a note with our phone numbers and an apology. (The owners wouldn't find the note for two years.) We were on our way to finish our record—we had dug ourselves out.

Back at the studio we finished the vocals and John mixed the record in a matter of days. He used Nirvana's *Nevermind* as an example of impeccable sequencing. That album was only a few years old at the time, so it was still the template for something incendiary. We put "Dig Me

Out" first, followed by "One More Hour" (a song that featured a riff I came up with after listening to Gang of Four's album *Entertainment* on repeat). Third was "Turn It On." John's baseball analogy was that you put your top three batters first. He also had an idea that there was an imaginary headphone listener named Jenny and that you should give her some sort of treat, something just for her, for that space in between her ears, like a secret message. So any time we added any little overdub or sonic Easter egg—Janet ended up playing one of the space heaters as a percussion instrument on "Heart Factory"—we'd think of her. I think that's how "Jenny" ended up as a song title on the record.

We really had no perspective as to what the record sounded like. Fellow Seattle producer Phil Ek and Fugazi's Brendan Canty both stopped into the studio on different days. Brendan heard a song called "Not What You Want" and said he thought it was great. They each commented that they liked the record and gave us generally positive feedback. But we had no idea. We left with a cassette of the album that John dubbed for us.

For the artwork, Janet had the idea of doing a take on *The Kink Kontroversy*. Something classic and clean. We had John Clark come over to Janet's house and take the photos, each emulating our respective member of the British band. For the back we used a Robert Maxwell photo, an outtake from a *Rolling Stone* shoot that we had done. We didn't make a video. We got out on the road.

When *Dig Me Out* was released, we toured in a light blue Ford Econoline van, listening to Armistead Maupin's *Tales of the City* on tape. Our friend Tim Holman, the one and only crew member, would sell T-shirts and help load the gear. Because he was the only male on the tour, some club employees felt more comfortable talking to him. He became our default interlocutor at times and also bore the brunt of people's confoundment. One night Tim got punched out by a security guy as he attempted to let him know it was okay for people to come onstage and dance. Corin decided to write a zine while we traveled called *Hey Soundguy*. She took a picture of every house sound person we encountered, told a short story about them, and wrote a review of both their performance and their personality. The zine featured three women; the rest were men. In one club, we were told that the room was shaped like the inside of a speaker and that we should face our amps directly toward Janet. When we refused, we were met with astonishment that we wouldn't change the ways we had always done things in order to fulfill this guy's wet dream of a perfect-sounding room.

During a gas stop, Tim came back from the station with a copy of *Time* magazine. Sleater-Kinney was in there, our record reviewed. Here we were in the middle of the country, in the middle of nowhere, just four of us in a stinky twelve-passenger van, and we could read about ourselves. This was not underground or provincial, but substantial, like a territory, like a country, like America. We climbed back into the van and drove to our next show.

Our success was more critical than commercial. We seemed to appeal to cultural influencers and pundits but we were too scary for the mainstream, our songs too strange. It was unnerving to have a spotlight on us, especially as Corin and I were struggling offstage. She was dating Lance and very much in the blissed-out state of being in love. Meanwhile, Janet and I, in a fit of righteousness and ridiculousness, had inexplicably banned him from all the shows on the *Dig Me Out* tour. This only made their relationship stronger and the two of them more resolute as a couple; it was them versus us, them versus the world. I don't exactly know why we banished Lance, except perhaps that we were scared of any outside influence or distractions. We wanted the fire to stay insular and didn't want his opinion, one that clearly mattered to Corin. Lance's exile made Corin angrier, pushed her further away. Resentment grew.

We did a handful of shows in the Pacific Northwest and in England, opening up for the Jon Spencer Blues Explosion. The Blues Explosion were a swaggering trio of dark-haired men led by the dashing and bellicose Jon Spencer. They played deconstructed, blown-out blues music that sounded tight and garbled, like it had been sucked through a straw. They were self-referential in their songs, every tune a lit-up marquee for themselves. The guys in the band were kind, jocose, intelligent. Jon was a physical performer and I took notes. He was a rubber band onstage, taught, wiggly, unpredictable. I give him credit for teaching me to stretch before I played. I liked the way the performance had an athletic, workmanlike quality to it, a feat to execute and to land.

Playing with JSBX was also the first time we were placed in a context that took us outside our Pacific Northwest heritage. They were from New York, with a decidedly hipper, more urbane fan base. One evening we were mistaken by a backstage security guard as groupies and nearly not let into our own dressing room. When we took the stage that night, Corin said, "We're not here to fuck the band, we *are* the band." At our show opening for JSBX at La Luna in Portland, I grew agitated at their crowd's indifference toward us and kicked the microphone stand into the audience. Jon voiced his dissatisfaction at my puerile behavior, more aware than I was that there is a difference between conjuring a sense of danger and actually harming someone. But I wanted our shows not just to be galvanic, I wanted to destroy the room. More than that, I wanted to obliterate myself, to unlock and uncork the anger, to disappear into the sound and into the music. In subsequent years when I kicked my legs out toward the crowd or swung my guitar close to the heads in the front row, it was about trying to physically harness the moment, to crash into strangers in a horrible but ecstatic impact, a shared bruising.

The shows on the *Dig Me Out* tour were getting bigger. But Corin and I were fighting harder. It came to a head in Austin. Janet and I had ganged up on her, vilifying Lance as if he were an interloper. At our Houston show, Corin and I fought in the dressing room, and just before we got onstage I called her a bitch. Right as the house music was turned down, I leaned over to apologize, hoping to salvage our onstage chemistry, and Corin said, "Get the fuck away from me." The mic was on. We started the show. I don't know if anyone heard. I was always so relieved to be in a band whose music could obliterate the before, tear through the moment and rip it to shreds. So that insult came and went, at least onstage. But after the set ends, you have to return to whatever state you were in. The animosity and sadness can only be suspended.

Corin and I were barely speaking. When we pulled off the highway to look for a hotel that night, she got out of the van at the off-ramp and started walking. No phone, no tour itinerary. She found her own hotel.

So much of the music we played was about peril and subsequent survival, but things had started to feel unsafe between us. Instead of our relationship and friendship being the antidote to our hurt, it was another element that added to the music's volatility, which made the shows exciting but made touring and being in the band as emotionally charged as our songs. We came to a fragile truce. I didn't want to lose Corin; it wasn't worth it. It was scary to think that we had journeys outside the band. *The Hot Rock* would speak to that. I consciously worked on being not just a creative partner but also a friend to Corin, a dependable ally and a confidante. Eventually, when Corin and Lance got married, I was the one she asked to give their wedding toast.

———

In the winter of 1997, we set off to London to begin a six-week tour, our first ever of Europe, to promote *Dig Me Out*. Helium, a band from Boston featuring the fantasy-driven lyrics and inventive guitar playing of Mary Timony, would open for us nearly the entire time. There were five of them and five of us. We bonded immediately and were inseparable for the remainder of the trip.

Tour started with a heap of excitement and a shaggy-haired English tour manager named Shane. "Think of me as your mother, your sister, your friend, your lover," she said to us right out of the gate. Her face was gaunt, a contrast of bony protrusions and deep creases. Incessantly calling us "dear" and "hon," she was somehow both Keith Richards and a full-time nanny. Or, rather, she was maternal toward me and Corin. With Janet, on the other hand, Shane was brusque, treating her like the hired help—a workhorse, a mule charged with helping to carry the load. Meanwhile, Corin and I were coddled—she wouldn't let us lift a finger. The disparity in how Shane approached us was becoming internecine for the band. After a spate of shows in France, including a night in Paris during which we drunkenly roamed the streets and Corin vomited in a cab and was kicked out by the driver before she could retrieve her fallen passport, we fired Shane. This was before the formation of the European Union, when each border required documentation. Now not only did we no longer have a tour manager, but one of us was unable to travel on to Spain.

Corin and our friend Chad, who was ostensibly along to sell merch but was more of a party planner, stayed behind in France to pay a visit to the U.S. consulate. They would meet up with us in Barcelona once the new passport was sorted. Meanwhile, Janet drove me and only me, along with all the equipment, in our rental van from England. With the steering wheel and gear shift on the right-hand side, we traveled precariously along the mainland-European highways, ones oriented like U.S. roads. Only two-thirds of a band and minus a leader, we felt as lopsided as our vessel.

In the end, it turned out that our madcap drive to Barcelona was for naught; we arrived in the city to find that, due to lack of ticket sales, our two Spanish shows had been canceled. With nothing but time, we suddenly found ourselves on holiday in Spain, visiting unscheduled but breathtaking cities like San Sebastián and missing our loved ones, with whom we had never traveled to places like this and possibly never would.

When tour started up again, back in France no less, we were introduced to our new tour manager, Camile. A Dutchman with frizzy hair the color of orange soda, he had a penchant for walking around in nothing but a towel. But Camile could speak four languages, helpful when crossing borders, and he took charge of the band and tour without being divisive. Plus, compared to Helium's beret-wearing, 1960s-era Paul McCartney look-alike of a road manager, who serenaded Janet over karaoke (with a Wings song) and French-kissed her in the hallway of a German hotel, Camile's steadiness and professionalism were a relief.

The tour stretched on for weeks. To this day it is the longest single tour I've ever been on and certainly the most debauched. Chad and I watched porn in our shared hotel room at night, which aired for free and was the only thing we could understand without the aid of subtitles. We lay in our underwear in adjoining twin beds, half turned on, half wanting to make out, but instead talking about how we missed our girlfriends back home. Along with Helium, we would go to late-night dance clubs after playing shows during which we'd slammed a round of whiskey shots delivered to us onstage before the encore. In Hamburg we went to a peep show where a dancer made this offer to Janet: "I'll lick your pussy, twenty dollars." (Janet declined.) We smoked cigarettes and weed, when available, ate copious amounts of chocolate and cheese, and fell asleep mostly tipsy if not outright drunk. On one long drive, in a fit of giddiness and in the spirit of sisterhood and spreading cheer, Corin and I convinced Janet to throw a mixtape out the van window. It was a cassette she'd been listening to nonstop, made for her by a friend, a boy she was trying to no longer have a crush on. That boy was Elliott Smith. I still think about that tape, flung, and how I urged it to be so. Gone.

Since I had never before traveled to Europe, I tried to make the most of the trip, treating it like both a vacation and a reconnaissance mission. Despite not going to sleep until three or four a.m., when the tourist destinations opened in the mornings, I would cram in an hour or two of sightseeing before we had to leave for the next city. I climbed up and down the roughly five hundred steps of the Cologne Cathedral and the four hundred steps of Gaudí's Sagrada Família in Barcelona (only upon completion of the ascent did I realize there was the option of an elevator); both endeavors caused cramping and limited mobility the next day. I went to the Anne Frank House, the Louvre, Sacré-Coeur, the Kunsthalle, and museums ranging from the British to the Van Gogh to a marionette museum in Switzerland. I bought art books and keychains, wine and postcards. I purchased prints of buildings and animals, rolling them up and stuffing them into shipping tubes that I had to keep track of for the rest of my travels. Only one, a nineteenth-century illustration of a giraffe from the Musée National d'Histoire Naturelle in Paris, made it home. It hangs in my bedroom to this day, the only keepsake from my valiant effort to binge on culture, to see and experience Europe in a nearly sleepless watercolor-like daze, wondering if I'd ever get a chance to again.

People often ask me about groupies on tour, about whether I had random and meaningless and super-hot sex. The answer is no. To all of it. We never had groupies. Writing that sad little sentence, I wish we *had*, just so instead I could have written, "Yes, of course we had groupies! Endless, countless numbers of groupies. A cornucopia of groupies, groupies coming out of my ears, groupies for days." Sure, we had fans who displayed emotions similar to a crush or were effusive enough to want hugs or to bring us gifts, who might even be bold enough to ask us on a date or perhaps scream "I love you" from the relative anonymity of a dark theater. But no one who waited outside the venue after the show or who we ran into later in the night at a nearby bar was someone any of us might end up going to bed with. Call it lack of opportunity or lack of imagination, but, to be honest, it was mostly lack of interest. Corin was with Lance from the *Dig Me Out* tour on, and Janet and I were in relationships on and off for most of our touring and band life.

But I'll admit, for the sake of seeming even a little less pitiful, there were two times I made out with people on the road. The first was in that summer of 1998 when Sleater-Kinney was finishing up the touring cycle for *Dig Me Out* in Europe. We were in Glasgow, which we'd flown into for a stretch of UK dates. We had a lot of friends who played music in that city, so we met up with members of Belle and Sebastian, Mogwai, the Yummy Fur, and Bis at a local bar. We danced and drank and sat around a big table laughing and talking until late. We were beyond drunk, all of us. Someone had handed out shots of Aftershock, a cinnamon-flavored and candy-red alcohol. I watched my friends getting handsy and loose with one another, leaning in, staying too long, staring too hard. When the bar closed, we all stood out on the street awaiting taxis. And it was there, in front of everyone, that I made out with a guy from one of the bands; he had a shaved head and looked like a footballer. I climbed into the taxi alone. Back in my hotel room, the room dipped and wobbled; I threw up repeatedly in the middle of the night. I was so hungover the next day that I couldn't get out of bed until we left for our show in Edinburgh at three o'clock in the afternoon.

I've seen pictures from that debauched event: my face is puffy, shiny, and bright red atop my body, like an emergency vehicle light; my eyes are glazed. If getting drunk to the point of vomiting is what it takes to be brave enough to put my mouth against an acquaintance and colleague in front of all our mutual friends, I'm going to say it might not be worth it.

The next time I had a dalliance on tour, there was some improvement in my overall decorum, though that might have been part of the problem as well.

In 2005, there was a woman I had a crush on, Melissa, an artist who lived in Los Angeles. We had been sending text messages and talking on the phone for the few months since we'd met briefly in Portland. And there came to be a sort of inferred agreement that we'd hang out when Sleater-Kinney played in L.A. during *The Woods* tour. After the concert and as planned, Melissa and I ended up back in my hotel room, which, luckily, I wasn't sharing with anyone else. Perhaps I had even optimistically asked for the "single." (We shared rooms on tour in order to save money. But because of an odd number of band and crew, we had a single room that we kept in rotation among Corin, Janet, and myself so that we each might have some alone time. It was appropriate to request this room if, say, your significant other was visiting or, as in my case, you were single and hoping to experience your first legitimate tour hookup.)

But here was the problem: Melissa and I had never really spent time together in person. And we were both shy. So, instead of getting back to
the room and throwing her on the bed, or her throwing me on the bed,
or us mutually throwing ourselves onto the bed, we talked. We talked
about our families, our work, our friends, our childhoods. As I grew more
tired I kept thinking, How much more information about former pets'
names and our parents' college experiences might need to be discussed
before we touch tongues? Apparently, *a lot* more. At four a.m., I put on
my pajamas and sat on the bed. By now it seemed obvious that Melissa
and I were going to embark on something less like the film *9½ Weeks* and
more like a sleepover I'd had at age nine and a half. When at last we had
shared every detail of our existence short of our Social Security numbers,
we stopped talking. We were lying down at this point, facing each other,
our bodies almost touching but not quite. Then, it happened. I'm not
certain if it was intentional or if we merely bumped into each other's faces
as we fell asleep, but as the morning light crept in through the cracks in
the curtains, our lips touched. An hour later, the alarm went off.

Those are my tour hookup stories.

Suffice it to say, being single while in a band is not the recipe for
opportunity that one might think; rather it is often a recipe for loneliness. But having a relationship is not easy, either. Being on the road,
recording, doing press tours, so much of a musician's life involves distraction and distance; it requires a total recalibration of what constitutes
home and stability. Finding a partner who understands the vicissitudes
of travel is challenging. A nomadic life fosters inconsistencies and contradictions within you, a vacillation between loneliness and needing
desperately to be left alone. To someone who misses you, and whom you
miss, bridging that space between togetherness and apartness, literally
and figuratively, can be brutal.

Here's one way not to go about attempting to diminish the distance: Obsessively call your girlfriend, who is eleven years older than you, crying and telling her you hate being on tour. Rack up more than $1,000 in pre–cellphone calling card fees on various payphones because you are hopelessly in love, willing to ditch everything for this person, and paranoid that she will go back to dating men while you are away. Get so worried that you walk into a family-run restaurant—perhaps the *only* restaurant—in the town of Lokev, Slovenia (population: around 1,000), ask to borrow their cordless phone, and call your girlfriend some more (sticking them with an international long-distance bill). Write lugubrious, handwritten love letters that compare thee to a summer's day. Drive your bandmates crazy by quoting your older girlfriend all the time and only reading books or listening to music that she has recommended. Now your bandmates are practically begging you to dump her. But, guess what, she dumps you. Of course she does. This girlfriend, who also plays music but who is not as successful as you in this field, you think she wants to hear how sad you are to have an album that is blowing up?! She doesn't. Months later you are still angry and confused and for the first time very, very heartbroken. You freak out and drive to her house one morning and place a bag containing every letter she ever wrote you on her doorstep. Then you write songs for what will become *The Hot Rock*, songs about a love that is so airless, it's suffocating. Songs about wanting to steal your heart back from someone you feel never deserved it. And thus begins a cycle, of falling in love and then getting hurt, or hurting someone else by falling out of love with them. About trying to maintain closeness despite geographical disparities, then finding inspiration from all the ways you feel splintered and separate, hurt and broken. So, this is one version, and not a pretty one, of being young and in a band and trying to be in a relationship. This is the version in which being gone and busy eats at you because you are scared of being left even though you are the one who is technically always leaving.

Skip ahead a few years and there is a new version of trying to have a relationship while being a touring musician: this time, the person is the best thing you've ever had. This woman is your age; she is smart and talented and kind and all your friends love her—you joke that they love her more than they love you. (You think this might still be true to this day.) Your methodology of making it work with this one is together-ness. She joins you on tour, she travels the world alongside you, you feel like a team. You swim with her in the fjords of Norway, you lie beside each other on the sand in Miami Beach, you walk the streets of Mexico City taking countless pictures of each other and of the sights; there is a brightness to it all. And yet there is also a glare, an irritation, causing you to blink and squint. When do you ever get to be alone? To think, to read, to reflect, to not have to be "on," to do nothing, to just . . . be. This version turns out not to be working either; there is not enough separation between you and her. She needs her own version of a life, to be her own protagonist. You move with her to California, she has a fel-lowship at Stanford. While living in the Bay Area, you write songs for *The Woods*, songs about America, freedom, longing, depression, suicide. You start to shut down, and off. You both move back to the Northwest but you feel doomed. It is one of your hardest breakups, a real tearing away—throwing away—of comfort. *The Woods* is out and though you don't know it yet, it's going to be your last album for a long while. For over a decade. So you don't get to write songs about this person; there are no more melodies to write. Without putting it to music, you have to figure out why you couldn't make this one work.

CHAPTER 13

THE HOT ROCK

The recording of *The Hot Rock* was an enervating experience. It sucked us dry. We had decided to work with producer Roger Moutenot, who recorded Yo La Tengo's *I Can Hear the Heart Beating as One*, an album all three of us admired. Our other albums had been recorded in a matter of days, but we scheduled three and a half weeks at Avast! Recording Co. in Seattle. In some ways, those first three albums felt like purges: we'd just go into the studio and bang out the songs; it was all about capturing a feeling, a crude aural bloodletting. But Moutenot was a producer. He labored over amp sounds and mic placement. And the songs were strange. Whereas *Dig Me Out* had a singular voice, the songs on *The Hot Rock* had two competing narratives, like a conscious and subconscious battling it out. Each song told two stories, the guitars each played a lead. All that was coherent and blunt about *Dig Me Out* atomized on *The Hot Rock*.

It's a labyrinthine record, sad, fractious, not a victory lap but speaking to uncertainty. The opening line of the first song (a song without a real title— "Start Together" was a working title referring to the fact that we literally started together, as opposed to I don't know what, staggering

in at different times) was "If you want, everything's changing." And it
felt like it was.

Whereas the band all stayed together when we'd recorded *Dig Me
Out*, this time around Corin and Janet lived in separate rooms at an
unassuming and generic extended-stay hotel. Meanwhile, I made myself
a temporary resident at the Crown Hill home of Ben and Kathy Gold-
farb and their three children. I was friends with Kathy's sister, who had
made the recommendation. Yet again, the band was dealing with a limited budget, and I was still young enough that the idea of crashing for
free at someone's house for nearly a month felt acceptable. While I grew
closer to my hosts—taking their kids to plays and the zoo and eating
breakfast with them before they left for school, talking with Ben and
Kathy late into the night, trying yet again to create a sense of family and
belonging—I rarely saw Janet or Corin outside of the studio. We arrived
at Avast! each day with a sense of trepidation, not knowing the prevail-
ing mood or what anyone was thinking or feeling.

A great source of the fissure and insecurity was that Roger thought
Corin was the star of the band—and certainly I would never deny
Corin's importance, or that her voice was part of what defined or made
this band—but we'd always been a trio. He was delicate with her, careful. Janet and I often felt like the backing players. Nonetheless, Moutenot
loved my guitar work and he procured some of my favorite sounds,
clean and distinct. He was definitely given the most challenging of our
material—only a handful of those songs had a singularity, most of them
sound schizophrenic, but he found a way to make that disjointedness
sound pretty, or at least listenable. In the end, *The Hot Rock* succeeded
in assuaging our worst fear, which was that we'd try to replicate *Dig
Me Out* but ultimately fail. Instinctively we knew that to avoid this
trap and skirt comparisons to our last record we had to create some-

thing completely different and unexpected. The critics couldn't fall back on, "This sounds like *Dig Me Out* except for . . . ," because it didn't sound like it at all. Though I knew we'd assembled a different beast, I remember leaving the studio with little sense of what we had done.

We asked Miranda July to film a video for the song "Get Up," the closest thing we had to a single, though by mainstream standards it sounded like something from a distant planet. On a brutally cold morning, the ground stubborn and unyielding from frost and freeze, we gathered outside Olympia at the farm of Vern Rumsey from the band Unwound. Despite having wanted to make a record decidedly different from its predecessors, it wasn't until the twenty or so young women who had gathered to be in the video first heard "Get Up" blasted through the stereo that I realized achieving that goal might be jarring to our listeners. Gone, at least for the moment, was the unrelenting throttle; in its place was weirdness and wonder. It was no less intense, but its melodic interstices, its winding and dual storytelling, allowed the listener to find places to sit within the songs. If *Dig Me Out* had been a punch, *The Hot Rock* was the reach of a desperate hand. We hoped people would latch on.

The video is as strange and avant-garde as anything we've ever done. Miranda's vision and sensibility were perfect for interpreting the song and the band at the time. A group of girls hold hands and walk through a field, picking Janet and Corin and me up from where we lie in the tall grass. There are flashes of light, of meteors. Corin's lyrics vacillate between the metaphysical and the primal. The video expresses an interior landscape of hope, promise, and mystery. Any major label at the time would have rejected it immediately; it was more art gallery than MTV. It was the first video we would show the world.

———

Barely a week into the *Hot Rock* tour, I was enjoying a rare moment of
downtime at Amoeba Music on Haight Street in San Francisco, dig-
ging through a bin of records, when I reached toward the middle of the
stack and was struck by a feeling of electricity in the middle of my spine.
I remember thinking, *This couldn't possibly be good.*

As we continued on to L.A. and then started heading east along the
bottom of the country, it got to the point where I flinched every time
the van ran over a pothole or a bump. The relative smoothness and
steadiness of the highway offered a reprieve, but when we entered a city,
I would wince and cry every time we rounded a corner. I felt like a
fragile eggshell in the backseat, frustrated that I had to be coddled.
There is little room for vulnerability on tour—it's very much about survival. And one person's weakness is annoying, a burden for everyone
else. All the energy and attention felt diverted toward me, focusing on
my back, how I was holding up. It wasn't a position I wanted to be in,
nor to put anyone else in.

By the time we reached New Orleans, I was in horrible pain. My
upper spine felt brittle, like it might just split in two. Every brick we
drove over as we passed through the French Quarter sent a jolt of pain
through my body. Backstage at the Howlin' Wolf, I hung from the
doorjamb. I was doing this because a club employee had recommended
it, to elongate my spine as much as possible. Everyone I met was suddenly a back expert. Do this, don't do that, take this, don't take that,
knot yourself into a pretzel, reach up like you're trying to pet a cloud,
squat, bend, lie down, sit. The discussion and input became as agoniz-
ing as the pain itself.

We had never played in New Orleans, except years before at a house party. This was our first proper show in a city we all were eager to perform in. But three songs into the show, I couldn't play another note. My guitar felt burdensome and crushing. I turned around to Janet; I was crying. That was it. We walked offstage.

Our plan was to rent a Lincoln town car—ostensibly more comfortable than our van, with a couch-like backseat I could lie on to convalesce—and drive to Athens, Georgia, where our next show was. The van and our crew went ahead. I felt like a baby, callow and infantile, being chauffeured by my bandmates. We drove the eight hours to Athens, where Corin read aloud to me while I bathed at the hotel. Generous as her act was, this *wasn't* tour—this was charity.

The following morning I went to a walk-in emergency clinic. Within minutes of examining me, the doctor told me I had torn ligaments in my upper spine and that if I didn't stop playing and touring, I would only further injure myself. I was relieved, but I also felt like a kid who was about to get in trouble. I had to tell everyone what the doctor said. Our booking agent had to cancel the rest of the shows. Janet and Corin suddenly had an expanse of time ahead of them, unstructured and unplanned, with no financial gain. I had let everyone down. We'd have to reschedule.

The next day I was on a flight home. I spent the following three weeks on my back, lying on my hardwood floors watching movies, seeing the action from that low-down, sideways perspective. I would go from the floor to a bathtub filled with Epsom salts and back to the floor. I would ice, then apply moist heat, then lie motionless. Friends brought me food. My cat Hector perched on me like furniture. It was unglamorous and anticlimactic. It wasn't Patti Smith breaking her neck because she fell from the stage, it was me rummaging for records and snapping like a twig. It was the first time that my body rebelled against the touring lifestyle, though it certainly would not be the last. I'm sure it was an amalgamation of stress and perhaps the change from my lighter Gibson SG to a much weightier hollow-body Rickenbacker.

But that shouldn't really matter. I felt ridiculous. And the injury changed the momentum and started a precedent of me always having a problem on tour. Touring for me just meant another visit to an emergency room. I've been to doctors and hospitals all over the world: Berlin, Leicester, Denver, Seattle. This, by the way, is not a brag.

CHAPTER 14

HELP

There are many good reasons to get a manager—such as having someone to help you negotiate with record labels, or do damage control when a recalcitrant band member bails—but we thought most didn't apply to us. We weren't irresponsible or uncommunicative. We genuinely liked one another and therefore didn't need a middleman to rescue us from the terrible task of having to talk to one another. And we weren't drug addicts or alcoholics. Those are the artists or bands who can't survive without a manager, and whose manager acts as pseudo-parent or even babysitter. We had started out doing everything on our own, from booking tours to sending out our records to be reviewed. And though we eventually had a label and booking agent, we were successful without having to employ a larger, potentially cumbersome team; eventually it became more difficult to imagine integrating someone into our infrastructure whom we'd all like and respect. Plus, it seemed inconceivable to give someone money for a job we were capable of doing.

But there are also much less dire reasons to have a manager, reasons that may have been useful to us but that we willfully ignored, or were just too stubborn or parsimonious to try. At a certain point, you have your label, and the five to ten people at the label with whom you work; you have your foreign labels and their personnel; you have your publishing company, your PR firm, a booking agent, a lawyer, an accountant. The manager is a very useful point person, someone to act as a veritable funnel, an organizer and translator of information, making it easier to make well-informed and stress-free (or less stressful) decisions.

Sleater-Kinney never allowed ourselves that luxury. We divvied up tasks among ourselves, from taxes to travel arrangements. We were three very capable people who liked the various business roles, so taking on this added responsibility for the most part didn't feel like a burden. But there were also times when we needed help, and it would have been advantageous to have someone uniformly on our side. Three is a volatile number for a creative endeavor and partnership. It's always uneven. It requires equality in order to achieve steadiness. When there is synchronicity and harmony, it's electric, a condensed energy, impenetrable. But more often than not it's two against one, an incessant ganging up, with the dominance and alliances constantly shifting. I talked with Corin about Janet, Janet and I talked about Corin, and Corin and Janet talked about me. As unified as we were onstage or (mostly) during recordings, we had disparate opinions about success and compromise, varying values and goals. A fourth, outside person might have been the voice of reason, someone to tip the scales in a more defined direction, to provide the clarity we couldn't always see from our cylindrical world.

Corin, Janet, and I had formed such a stubbornly insular unit of a band that there were very few music-business people we trusted, and even fewer whom all three of us agreed on. Only two people made it through the tough exterior and our collective agreement.

Julie Butterfield was one of the first people I met in Olympia, where she had moved from Minneapolis. If you weren't in a band in Olympia, you were running a label, and Julie had a small imprint called Skinny Girl that had put out a 7-inch single or two. Julie brought a refreshing and unprecedented sense of expertise and professionalism to Olympia; she had a big-city sensibility (when someone from Minneapolis has a "big-city sensibility," you know how small Olympia is). In 1995, when Corin and I had finished recording *Call the Doctor*, we wanted to send it out to press people. So I contacted Julie, who gave me a printout with names and addresses and told me which writers might be amenable to our music. She was savvy and seemed in possession of information we couldn't possibly have had access to otherwise—not without a fully staffed label or manager, not in a town that was essentially in a media blackout and that considered doing press almost an act of "selling out." Julie became our publicist for nearly the entirety of our career. She was a good sounding board and always had our best interests in mind. She understood the context from which we came, not only our ambitions but where we weren't willing to compromise. She was a friend and support system, an ally.

Bob Lawton showed up when *Call the Doctor* and our self-booked tour started to earn us wider recognition. He was the booking agent for Sonic Youth and Yo La Tengo, both bands we looked up to. Bob was a real old-school New Yorker—he'd seen a lot, lived hard, and had the accent, stories, and sardonicism to prove it. We were an unlikely pairing. He wasn't from our world; he didn't know the preciousness or politics of Olympia or the Pacific Northwest, and he didn't really care. This meant he unequivocally fought for us, and he didn't feel limited by the unstated but very ossified and encoded rules of the punk or indie scene. That doesn't mean he wasn't ethical—he was. But he was driven and he instilled in us a sense of worthiness. He loved our music and he wanted people to hear it.

Bob was very opinionated, tenacious with the bookers at clubs, and he knew far more than we did. Before him, we would feel blindsided by events or next steps, whereas Bob could look at the coming album and the year ahead and assess exactly what needed to happen. As a booking agent he was pretty typical at the time: very full service, very philosophical. He wanted us to play smaller or medium-size venues and sell them out, to make sure there was a sense of urgency surrounding the show, a sense of discovery and exclusivity, so that next time we could play a bigger venue because everyone at that first show would tell their friends what they had seen. Bob had a deep connection to our band and he was protective of us. Over time he developed an almost avuncular affection for each of us individually, and we admired him and trusted him immensely. He booked us right up until he retired, just before *The Woods*.

Left largely on your own, you often turn on one another. Tour was taking its toll. I found it difficult to maintain friendships and relationships in the age of the postcard and the payphone. I spent much of my time trying to tether myself back to home, but often when I got home I found I had less to return to. Every gas station stop was an excuse to dial out from a grimy payphone, just to hear a few minutes of a familiar voice or at least their outgoing voicemail message to get you through the next three hours in the van. Returning home at the end of a tour, I would enter an airless house that had collected an eerie dust from misuse. Everything was exactly how I had left it, yet I felt like a stranger. That feeling of alienation was alleviated when I adopted two cats from the Olympia animal shelter. I named them Hector and Lyle. They provided an excuse to have someone stay at the house while I was gone, so when I came home there was evidence of the house having been lived in, comfort in the daily rituals I imagined took place while I was gone, someone had marked time. Most of all, there were two little creatures to greet me.

After a European tour where harsh words were exchanged and a plate of food was thrown, followed by a Chunnel ride during which Corin did not speak to me or Janet, we decided we might need to bring in some extra help. Enter Susan and Nina, a couple of therapists who were couples therapists, and also happened to be a couple. They tag-teamed their way through therapy sessions. Needless to say, they were in Olympia, and recommended to us by a handful of friends who were also seeing them. Susan was the taller, more formidable of the two—short dark hair, deep voice. Nina had short blond hair, bright eyes. They were sort of like good cop, bad cop. Susan was the tough-love counselor. Nina was the empath. They used their own relationship for examples, and as a result, details of their personal histories are permanently lodged in my brain. I'm not sure how useful it is to know that Nina was once married to a professional football player.

Together, band and therapists, we became a ten-legged lover working through our issues. The first thing we did was make a pie chart. We were each asked to illustrate how much of our life we wanted Sleater-Kinney to occupy, so we could understand how each of us might be approaching the band and its importance in our lives differently. As I looked down at my divided circle, it was the first clue I had that the band was something that represented a fair bit of anxiety for me as compared to Janet and Corin. My drawing indicated that Sleater-Kinney, and in particular touring, were something I wanted as part of the story, but perhaps not the entire story. In total, we attended two or three sessions, learning to speak in "I feel" statements, airing our grievances, crying, and learning a lot about Susan and Nina. We left with a set of rules that served us well: No evil-minded buddying up. No breaking up the band on tour. Always say you're sorry. And if someone calls an emergency meeting, you have to oblige.

Therapy gave us tools and pulled us back together, but ultimately it was still just the three of us. Therapy wouldn't diminish the number of times we'd get angry with one another, but now we at least knew we had to apologize. Of course, now that we'd aired our deepest fears and vulnerabilities, we also knew the quickest ways to hurt one another.

CHAPTER 15

ALL HANDS ON THE BAD ONE

The Hot Rock had been a difficult album to record and to take on tour. The songs were tortuous and challenging to play live, each instrument traveling down a different road. As a result, we felt disjointed.

The writing for our next record began between legs of the *Hot Rock* tour. We split the work between Janet's basement in Portland and mine in Olympia. These songs came out easy and rapid, like fast-drying glue putting us back together; we were in a hurry to return to something cohesive.

Corin had been playing in a side project called Cadallaca, a retro-sounding garage-rock trio with fake names and fake hair. She had come to enjoy the freedom of singing in character—male and female— and wanted to bring some of that vocal multidimensionality and nuance into our songs. Songs like "Ballad of a Ladyman" and "Milkshake n' Honey" were sung with a saucy detachment that I hadn't heard from her before.

Musicians, especially those who are women, are often dogged by the assumption that they are singing from a personal perspective. Perhaps it is a carelessness on the audience's part, or an entrenched cultural assumption that the female experience can merely encompass the known, the domestic, the ordinary. When a woman sings a nonpersonal narrative, listeners and watchers must acknowledge that she's not performing as *herself,* and if she's not performing as herself, then it's not *her* who is wooing us, loving us. We don't get to have her because we don't know exactly who she is. An audience doesn't want female distance, they want female openness and accessibility, familiarity that validates femaleness. Persona for a man is equated with power; persona for a woman makes her less of a woman, more distant and unknowable, and thus threatening. When men sing personal songs, they seem sensitive and evolved; when women sing personal songs, they are inviting and vulnerable, or worse, catty and tiresome. Whether Corin was singing from her own perspective or from someone else's, I never had to ask if she was okay. Her voice was torrential, a force as much as it was human.

The songs that comprised *All Hands on the Bad One* were full of proclamations and affirmations. Once again, we were in conversation first and foremost with ourselves and with each other. *All Hands* was a reset button. We returned to working with John Goodmanson; we sang about the experience of playing music as if it were brand new. There is a sense of rejuvenation on the album. But for the first time we were also reacting to specific events and politics instead of doling out a diffuse rage à la *Call the Doctor* and *Dig Me Out* or the dark yearning of *The Hot Rock.*

After years spent trying to distance ourselves from what felt like overly simplistic Riot Grrrl and feminist signifiers, attempting to eschew categories that seemed only to diminish or ghettoize the band and the music, sometimes the effort of pushing ourselves away felt like an act of self-amputation, self-effacement. It was also exhausting to continually try to separate who we were from what we made. And each time I wanted things to be transcendent, to disregard gender dynamics or sexism, those things reared their ugly heads. It's hard to divorce yourself from that conversation.

Especially at Woodstock 1999, when there was a reported rape and multiple allegations of sexual assault, and when "Show Me Your Tits" could have been the fest's unofficial slogan. (We responded to the latter with a tour T-shirt that said "Show Me Your Riffs," one that Corin and many of the fans wore around the release of the album.) This was our workplace: a concert, the music industry. Or later, while engaging in the camaraderie of a music festival in England called the Bowlie Weekender, when we found a note calling us "ladymen" affixed to the bulletin board on our chalet. Or attempting to talk about our music and the process of writing an album in an interview, then to read the article and see that the writer focused on what we were wearing or how we looked, discussed our gender, or made a sexist comment in the story.

This was the same time as the Spice Girls and "Girl Power." We knew there was a version of feminism that was being dumbed down and marketed, sloganized, and diminished. We wanted to draw deeper, more divisive lines. We wanted to separate ourselves from anything benign or pretty. One of my favorite songs that Corin has ever written, "Was It a Lie?", sounds so prescient now in the age of social media and the voracious news and gossip cycles. The song is about a woman whose videotaped death is replayed for the amusement of others.

Do you have a camera for a face?
Was she your TV show?
Was she your video?

A woman's pain, never private always seen

I want to close my eyes

I want to cut the wires

I want a day not made for you to see

We were never trying to deny our femaleness. Instead, we wanted to expand the notion of what it means to be female. The notion of "female" should be so sprawling and complex that it becomes divorced from gender itself. We were considered a female band before we became merely a band; I was a female guitarist and Janet was a female drummer for years before we were simply considered a guitarist and a drummer. I think Sleater-Kinney wanted the privilege of starting from neutral ground, not from a perceived deficit or a linguistic limitation. Anything that isn't traditional for women apparently requires that we remind people what an anomaly it is, even when it becomes less and less of an anomaly.

I will now take a moment to compile for you a representative sample of journalism about Sleater-Kinney. Most of these articles are actually trying to be complimentary—the authors just fell into common traps and assumptions.

> You can call them punk. You can call them chicks. In fact, you can call them anything. But whatever you do, just don't use that tired, worn phrase and call female trio Sleater-Kinney a riot grrrl band.
>
> Prior to the interview, the band's publicist even suggested that we refrain from asking the inevitable "women in rock" questions. But after listening to Sleater-Kinney's tender yet irate brand of punk, you almost can't help it. . . .
>
> (CNN, 1999)

But never does Sleater-Kinney sound forced, angry or sweet—the three words one most associates with all-women rock bands, and the three words that tend to hold women's music back from the kind of raw believability that characterizes more macho rock.

(Metroactive, 1999)

Post-Riot-Grrls Sleater-Kinney are a boy rock critic's wet dream. Not just because they sport that pouty, Salvation Army T-shirt-wearing look that drives those guys wild, but because SK's fifth album, *All Hands on the Bad One* (Kill Rock Stars), is the kind of complex, multifaceted work that sparks hours of tedious nerd-speak. Is it a self-important, jaded up-yours to their indie-rock peers? Is it a portrait of the young ladies as artists? Is it a song-by-song conceptual response to the Go-Go's *Beauty and the Beat*? The answer, more than likely, is yes to the third (the thematic cohesion is remarkable), but who cares? . . .

The trio blends synthesizers (!) and fuzzed-out boy-rock almost sweetly everywhere else—clues to the lay listener that there's more going on here than just some spoiled little tomboys postponing their entrance into the workforce. . . .

So the Y-chromosome-bearing, cardigan-and-chain-wallet-wearing set can pop open a six-pack of Mountain Dew, kick off the Chuck Taylors, and settle in for a night of fawning. Everyone else should take *All Hands on the Bad One* as evidence that Sleater-Kinney aren't some overrated one-trick indie artifact to be filed between Bikini Kill and Bratmobile—and proof to the boys that they're more than three hot chicks in low-rider cords.

(City Pages, 2000)

The four questions *Rolling Stone* asked us in a mini feature:

Who were your musical heroes growing up?

Were there female musicians who were particularly influential
on you? *[A follow-up, perhaps because Janet had answered the
previous question with "Joe Strummer"?]*

How has parenting affected your songwriting, Corin?

Have things changed for women musicians much during the
last decade?

(Rolling Stone, 2002*)*

Fortunately, their frequent lyrical challenges to gender roles didn't
devolve into rote male-bashing, and both sexes jumped and
bobbed with joyful abandon. It helped that the three were quick
with smiles, obviously enjoying the charged room.

(Washington Post, 1998*)*

The above were written by men and women. Obviously, it's easy to
internalize sexism.

You get the idea.

Critics were not as unified in their affection of *All Hands* as they had
been on the previous albums, nor as effusive and laudatory as they
would be about the later two. In fact, a weekly Seattle paper called *The
Stranger* decided to publish not one review but instead a *roundtable* on
All Hands on the Bad One. I read the issue in an Olympia coffee shop the
day before we started our tour for the album up in Seattle. And the next

night onstage, I thought about the negative criticism far more than I did the sold-out crowd. It was the last time I read a review.

Despite feeling vulnerable about the mixed feedback, in hindsight I appreciate the effort of the publication to engage its audience in a thoughtful and well-informed critique regarding a creative work. An entire roundtable! A divisive album! More and more I am glad that Sleater-Kinney had little universal appeal, that there were elements to our band that were essentially "deal-breakers." There was no middle ground; we were either loved or hated, but at least our music elicited a reaction and fomented conversation.

I think cultural criticism and long-form critique have their place and their purpose. But for a creator, it's so easy for the discussion surrounding a phenomenon to usurp the phenomenon itself. It's worse, of course, with comment sections on websites and blogs, particularly anonymous comments, or the incessant chatter and opinions on social media. Everyone gets to write a headline, and when you or the thing you do is being talked about, you get to *feel* like a headline—an addicting feeling for sure, but also a pernicious one. The discourse builds its own body, and it's usually a monster.

Although I will confess that *All Hands* has shaken out to be my least favorite Sleater-Kinney record, I will say that there are crucial moments on it that act as the connector between the first and second half of our catalog. There are times that a work exists for the sake of getting you to the next step, as a testing ground for ideas, for recognizing parts of your process that were theretofore unnoticed or undiscovered. Most of the other songs on the album were a continued expansion and stretching in our songwriting. There is the nod to classic rock in "Male Model," thick, sludgy riffs that hint at "Light Rail Coyote" on *One Beat* and much of *The Woods*. And a catchiness in the choruses of songs like the title track and "Leave You Behind" paid more attention to melody than we ever had in the past.

All Hands on the Bad One also illustrates the differences between how Corin and I approach lyric writing. While we often wrote the music collaboratively, we worked on the words separately. Whoever had brought in the original riff or song, or whoever came up with the vocal melody, was usually the one who figured out a theme, a subject matter. We responded to our environment in different ways. My narratives were often oblique, hers direct. She was bold; I described boldness. I read books about the Civil War and likened two obstinate people to the ironclad ships the *Monitor* and the *Merrimac*. "The Swimmer" was inspired by an interview with long-distance swimmer Lynne Cox and the way she described the ocean as being a world in which she felt the most herself, needing to escape in order to be found. Corin, on the other hand, took out her anger and alarm head-on. "#1 Must Have" dealt explicitly with the Woodstock 1999 violence. Contemptuous, sarcastic, using clever turns of phrase, she was able to shove back the listener with her voice. The song also explored the commodification and co-opting of the once-radical tenets of Riot Grrrl and punk rock feminism by the mainstream, their remnants echoed in hollowed-out and sellable phrases, divorced from any form of social justice or action. "You're No Rock n' Roll Fun" was about a certain kind of arrogant, self-serious indie boy. It was sassy and direct, with a Shangri-Las–style taunting, a ganging-up after having felt ganged-up on. It was retaliation you could sing along to.

I admired Corin for the way she wrestled our songs down to the ground with her vocal delivery, tamed them or took flight, could play with the tension between the guitar and vocal melody, could be as punchy and deliberate as the drums. She was masterful. Up until *All*

Hands, when I sang I often felt like the songs were on the verge of swallowing me. I didn't feel like that on guitar; my guitar could fight back in a way I never could with my voice. But *All Hands* was the first album where I start to sing above the surface of the song.

All Hands was certainly more accessible than its predecessor. These were songs that allowed us to focus on the task of performing. They were imbued with drama, the choruses sounded like choruses; we expanded the scaffolding and it made us a better live band. We had been operating from a place of sonic misanthropy in some ways, but *All Hands* also has frivolity and irony, a sense of humor despite all its seriousness and direct assessment of specifically tragic incidents. It brought the band back to the center but scraped enough from the outer edges of what we'd reached for to give us musical fodder and confidence for what would come next.

Live, we were tighter and more confident than ever, and the *All Hands* touring was energetic and mercifully free of injury.

By the time we went to Europe during the *All Hands* touring cycle, I had no illusions about tour as a vacation proxy. Climbing into the van in Amsterdam, my body knew what to do when it hit the seat: slump, readjust and sit up straight, slump again. Tour consisted of riding in the van for eight to ten hours a day depending on the distance between cities, a bottle of water and a bag of chips held between my knees, a book in my hands, nodding off to sleep then jerking awake, my body compressed and folded.

Our first show of the tour took place at the aptly named Dour Festival in Belgium. I didn't recognize any of the other bands who were playing, which meant one of two things: 1) The rest of the bands were from

Europe, or 2) They were bands from the United States who were only popular in Belgium. It was a show during which death from electrocution felt both certain and imminent. The rain was coming at us horizontally and much of the stage was wet, including our instruments. My guitar glistened with droplets like in a bad '80s hair metal video. It was so cold that I was dressed in layers, piling onto my body nearly everything I had packed in my suitcase. As a precautionary measure, the stage manager covered the monitors with large garbage bags, and in retrospect, I should have asked him to throw some plastic over me as well. We played to ten beer-drinking, poncho-wearing men and a lone poncho-wearing woman.

We arrived in Paris to play two shows (safely indoors) opening for Sonic Youth. A bit timid after the humiliation of the previous day, we started our set the first night feeling beat down, like we had to fight our way back. It took about half the set for my confidence to return, for the music to move through me without getting tripped up on the interlopers of doubt and nerves, to know the sound belonged within me.

My friends James and Ian from the Washington, D.C., band the Make-Up showed up with a small entourage of Parisians. They invited us to a party; I tried to convince Corin and Janet to join, but they weren't up for a late night. In the end it was only our sound guy, Juan, and I who ventured out. We arrived at a high-ceilinged apartment sparsely decorated save for two large wall mirrors and neon artwork atop the mantel. There were a handful of men milling around, drinking wine and smoking. There were only two other women present, who I assumed to be friends of the hosts, but who I was told were actually call girls.

As music played on the stereo speakers and dancing ensued, the atmosphere turned Dionysian. I sat on a sofa watching bodies become more entangled, turning from angles and lines to squiggles and waves.

I mentally riffled through the files of my Olympia experiences to find the right protocol for this situation. A futile exercise. Then I thought of the Left Bank in the early 1900s, about expats, Gertrude Stein, Pablo Picasso, Djuna Barnes, Colette. But this was a situation where knowledge was no match for experience. I wanted to come across as insouciant. I was in a rock band! I was on tour! I was at a sexy soiree in Paris! But I couldn't even figure out what to do with my face. I held my expression perfectly still, trying to appear neither overly curious nor mildly shocked. I soon realized the tension in my jaw was forming a grimace. In the end, all I could manage was the kind of shoulder dance moms do when they make shrimp scampi in the kitchen while drinking white wine and listening to Bruce Hornsby. I shimmied right out of the room, exited the apartment, and took a taxi back to the hotel.

The next day, Janet, Corin, and I went to the designer Marc Jacobs's apartment to help Kim Gordon out with a Sonic Youth video for the song "Nevermind (What Was It Anyway)." We were assigned roles as ambivalent party guests and told to sit around on various couches looking disinterested. We stared past the other guests or looked out the window until the boredom would become too great and one of us would stand up and leave the room, only to be replaced by another vacant-eyed partygoer. We shot for a few hours, the action easy to execute but the finesse and coolness hard to pull off without looking like I was trying too hard. It didn't help that I was wearing a too-tight, pale blue sweater that I'd purchased at a French department store the day before and a pair of office-employee slacks.

As if to cement my sense of humility, I stepped in dog shit right as we exited Marc's apartment. I spent the walk back to our hotel in search of puddles or serrated edges with which I could rid myself of my shameful, putrid secret.

Later in the tour, the band taped an Italian MTV interview in Verona under the famous balcony where Juliet stood gazing down at her beloved Romeo. Afterward, the three of us paid money to climb up that very balcony and gaze down at hundreds of non-Romeos, a.k.a tourists. (Not to say that we were anyone's idea of Juliets either, especially after a few weeks in the van.) I opened the guest book that sits at the top of the stairs. Instead of declarations of love worthy of Shakespeare himself, or at least worthy of posterity, I was met with drawings like the requisite cock 'n' balls and epistolary outbursts perhaps best saved for bathroom-stall confessionals.

All of these experiences summed up the disparities and vacillations that typify tour: the ridiculous and the sublime, the charming and the execrable. In a journal entry I wrote on the flight home, I noted that it felt like I had been gone for months instead of three weeks. *It's as if I'm wearing new skin, or rather that I hardly fit inside my old anymore, I feel stretched and distorted. The end of tour, it's almost like waking up in the hospital after an accident: Slowly you take stock of the damage, a cut, a scrape, maybe you discover a part that no longer functions properly.*

CHAPTER 16

ONE BEAT

In 2000, Corin called to tell me that we would need to take time off from the band—she was pregnant. I went into a momentary state of panic. What would I do without Sleater-Kinney? But also, who *was* I without this band?

The quest to answer that second question led to a manic state of traveling, working, and filling up my days, weeks, and months. I made plans. And then I made more plans. I became a full-fledged research assistant to my former sociolinguistics professor and mentor. I flew to Los Angeles to meet with my uncle's ex-wife, who was an executive at Paramount Studios; I thought perhaps I could be a production assistant and get into film and television work. I applied to be a substitute teacher in the Olympia School District, which apparently suffered a shortage of qualified applicants. So, with a bachelor's degree, five albums on my résumé, and years of touring experience, I was hired. I woke up at five a.m. two or three days a week, drove to a middle school or high school in town, and followed the teacher's instructions for their sub—me—which usually involved pressing play on A/V equipment in science, English, and history classrooms and showing the students a movie or

handing out pop quizzes. Within a few weeks I knew the drill: Walk
into class and write "Mrs. B" on the board because the kids were used
to everyone being married and having pronounceable names, and wear
a pair of high heels because otherwise most everyone thought I was a
new student.

When I wasn't "teaching," I acted in one of Miranda July's experi-
mental short films, which involved me sprawled out on a bed in a turtleneck while a long-haired cat preened around on a floral bedspread,
and I auditioned for and got a role in a local independent movie about
group therapy that essentially put a handful of women who were "acting" and "in character" through (excruciating) group therapy while they
filmed us. None of these activities told me specifically who I was or
who I would be outside of Sleater-Kinney, but they did speak to a new-
found confidence and intrepidness that I had not previously realized I
had. This respite from the band also highlighted a restlessness that I
found was hard to satiate. I quickly grew weary of stillness.

Olympia had been a valuable incubator, but by the time I was in my
late twenties, it felt decidedly claustrophobic. I had outgrown its perennial adolescence. The cyclical nature of a college town means a new
crop of fresh-faced eager hopefuls pour into and populate the city at the
same time that an older, more seasoned group, with new ambitions and
new sights in the crosshairs, moves away. At a certain point, I felt too
old to hang with the new recruits, too ambivalent toward the quirki-
ness that small-town DIY life engenders, too young to settle down, too
irked by the self-aware preciousness of it all. Art communities and
music scenes want to pretend like they don't care, but they will also tell
you louder and more frequently than anyone that they DON'T CARE.
These self-aware scenes are as cool as a secret handshake and a sly shared

gesture of recognition, but at some point I was done living inside the town equivalent of a wink.

A major turning point for me in my feelings about ambition and career came during the planning of Ladyfest, a festival that took place in Olympia in August 2000. As its website declared, Ladyfest was a "non-profit, community-based event designed by and for women to showcase, celebrate and encourage the artistic, organizational and political work and talents of women." As a volunteer for the festival, and part of a team of people attempting to raise funds, I attended planning meetings. Frustration was high, as a group of about twenty of us attempted to navigate and cater to everyone's needs and wishes, differences and ideologies. We were often at an impasse, inert from politeness (or passive-aggressiveness), no one wanting to take charge or declare themselves a leader. Despite our best intentions, we had the momentum and direction of a silk scarf being juggled by a mime.

During one of these meetings we talked about press for the festival. The team that was in charge of PR expressed open agitation and disdain that many of the media outlets were most interested in interviewing Sleater-Kinney. At the time, we were one of the biggest acts playing the festival, and certainly the most well-known active band associated with Olympia. Here I was in a group of women, allies, I thought, colleagues, and I felt like I was being shamed for the relatively modest success I had achieved. But instead of sticking up for myself, I apologized. I downplayed my level of enthusiasm for my own work and accomplishments, I expressed remorse for the fact that my band was considered separate from the community as a whole. And, truth be told, I did feel terrible. At least in that moment. I left the meeting with a pit in my stomach. Later, however, I was livid. And heartbroken.

I felt like I had been thrown under the bus and betrayed by my own gender.

As much as I love and loved Olympia, and owe so much of my musical upbringing to its ethos, it was a place I needed to leave. I never wanted to feel ashamed for striving, for desiring, for ambition. And I never wanted to judge another woman, or anyone, for that matter, for their own aspirations, even if they differed from my own.

When Corin's son was born, I began traveling to Portland more frequently so that we could write songs and I could hang out with her new baby, a boy named Marshall. I spent many hours on the couch catching up with Corin. I held Marshall in my lap, placing my lips on his downy, delightful infant head. I was downtrodden, bewildered, and ungrounded. I wanted to be closer to this feeling of home, of love. Portland seemed my only viable option if I wanted to keep the band intact and vibrant, and I did. In the fall of 2001—with 9/11 like a new sky over the country, a different air on our skin, changing the way we saw and felt everything—I decided to leave Olympia altogether.

I moved to an apartment in southeast Portland that October, with my cats Hector and Lyle, fresh from being cheated on and a subsequent breakup and in that post-9/11 mind-set, where all the structures you felt like you could count on now seemed tenuous. You acknowledged the unsteadiness and either braced yourself against it or let it transplant you somewhere else. I didn't go far. My new home was two hours south of my old one and only five miles from the border of the state I'd lived in my entire life.

Compared to Olympia, Portland seemed both cultured and urban. It felt like a real city because of how derelict it was, how many homeless people, how much garbage and grit. A city's scope could be measured then not by the number of good restaurants, coffee shops, and dog day-cares but by the quantity of problems it had. Its realness could be quantified by its deficits. And here the music scene had more than one center; it felt multifaceted, like you might not meet every single person, which is an obvious fact in most cities but not in small towns. I sensed a greater amount of drive and ambition in Portland that was still matched by many of the principles on which Sleater-Kinney had been built and founded. We remained far from the music industry centers of L.A. or New York, still able to create from the margins, and people here valued community, innovation, and the retention of artistic credibility.

Portland became a respite and a true hometown. Personally, as well as in Sleater-Kinney, I have always relied heavily on resetting. I venture out and take risks, but then I need to return to steadiness and calm. Portland has a nurturing quality, a placidity. For better or worse, it's a perennial but shyly hopeful city; if we had a gesture it would be a shrug.

When I'd visit Portland in the '90s, it had a seedy quality to it. Just watch Gus Van Sant's *Drugstore Cowboy* if you want to get a fairly realistic picture of some of the locals. Like Seattle before the dot-com boom, Portland—and the Pacific Northwest in general—still felt like a place people came to disappear. You can hear that heaviness in the music from that era, the sadness in Nirvana, Mudhoney, Crackerbash, the Wipers (who were from earlier years)—the sounds embodied the emotional equivalent of getting washed up on the beach somewhere. You can feel at the mercy of your surroundings in the Northwest, subsisting on dreariness until even your internal landscape feels soggy. It's depressing, and before the money came in, before the buildings started to reflect the bright ideas and optimism, that sadness was reflected back much more poignantly.

Writing songs after 9/11 felt treacherous. There wasn't much of a vocabulary other than fear and patriotism. Many people felt a growing anger and distrust toward the Bush-Cheney administration, yet public dissent or even questioning of the status quo was likened to treason. The Dixie Chicks' relatively mild comment admonishing George Bush while performing overseas would soon ignite vitriol, boycotts, and even death threats.

Yet the political landscape wasn't the only thing fueling our songwriting or the element that defined the sound on our next record. For one, it was the first time in the history of the band that all three members lived in the same city. Rather than me commuting to Portland for a matter of hours, or Janet and Corin driving up to Olympia for the day, we could retain both a prolonged intensity to the writing sessions but also work without the pressure of a time limit. In the past, if inspiration didn't strike, the next time we would all be together might be days or weeks away. But now we could take breaks when we got stuck or tired, or reconvene the next day. We had a new sense of continuity and momentum, ease and fluidity. And the short hiatus we had taken while Corin was pregnant instilled within us a *need* for Sleater-Kinney.

Janet lived off Hawthorne Boulevard, a street where hip met hippie, where vintage clothing and bead stores commingled. The front-cover album photos for *Dig Me Out* were taken in her living room. We'd been practicing in the basement of her one-story bungalow since the *Hot Rock* days. The interior color scheme of the house was garish and bold, Pepto-Bismol pink in one room, kelly green in another, landscape and animal paintings hung on the wall. There were sleek pleather sofas and chairs, and coffee-table art books. These rooms were as familiar as those in my own house. Across the smudged and graying linoleum of the kitchen, down a few steps where Janet had old newspaper clippings from the Portland Trail Blazers' one and only championship season stapled to the wall, past the washer/dryer and, finally, around a corner, was our practice space. It smelled of mold and cleaning supplies, dryer sheets and dust. Old carpeting and mattresses were affixed to the walls for soundproofing, along with a small chalkboard on which to write the song names. Now we stepped into it as if anew.

The riffs Corin and I were bringing in were charred and bluesy; Corin had one we called "Sympathy," partly as a nod to the Rolling Stones' "Sympathy for the Devil." There had been an article in a local paper about a coyote hopping a ride on the light-rail transit system, which we turned into a love song to Portland. "Combat Rock" was our version of a reggae song as done by the Clash, which of course was why we called it what we did. And we had a tune with a working title of "One Beat," which characterized its drum part.

We recorded *One Beat* at Jackpot! Recording Studio's original location on NE Morrison Avenue, with Larry Crane as the engineer and John Goodmanson again as producer. I've only cried once in the studio, and it was when Corin sang her vocals for "Sympathy," a song about her fears of losing her son when he was born premature, the anxious, tender, and frightening days he spent in the NICU. Janet and I sat on the couch behind the mixing console and held our breath. Corin did the song in a single take.

One Beat is often characterized as a "political" album, which speaks to how long it took for musicians—especially in the mainstream—to address or make sense of the xenophobia and jingoism that took hold of the culture post-9/11. *One Beat* was one of the earliest. Yet the common thematic thread on the record is less overtly political and more an exploration of faithlessness, of trying to uncover hope or meaning in a time that was very, very bleak. Certainly "Faraway" and "Combat Rock" address politics explicitly and deliberately, but the title track and "Sympathy" search for meaning in scars, using pain and wounds as a vernacular. The album spoke to a dismantling of old ways, of old loves, of old ideas.

We had stepped away from the band for only a moment but realized soon enough that we wanted to pour everything we had back into it. Sleater-Kinney is never a group I could be in with any sense of passivity; there is a deliberate, almost unseen force to it. We wanted to be a sonic call to action, anthemic, to either join in or get out, to be shaken from indifference—not only the listeners but ourselves.

Before the album was released, we were asked to open for Belle and Sebastian at the Daughters of the American Revolution Hall in Washington, D.C. It is a beautiful theater, a far cry from the rock clubs and venues we were used to playing. Every once in a while—mostly at festivals stocked with bands with incessant four-on-the-floor kick drum patterns and choruses and arrangements graspable both immediately and from a mile away—I would be reminded of how abrasive our band could sound, how harsh we could appear in a feather-wearing, beach ball–tossing, polite context. And really, there was no band who played more polite music than Belle and Sebastian. Knowing we had no way of winning over the delicate ears of their cardigan-wearing fans, we played our unreleased record, in its sequence and entirety, to the audience. None of our old songs would have likely been familiar anyway. In that ancient world of pre-cellphone-camera codependency and social media addiction, no one captured the moment.

One Beat was released in August 2002. We took a small and up-and-coming band from Akron called the Black Keys out on the road with us. It was unnerving to venture back into a world where we might yet again have a label or indexer placed before the term "band." We had spent years attempting to exist free of excess and arbitrary labels that were not descriptions of our music: female, indie, queer. Riot Grrrl, post–Riot Grrrl music. Now here we were with the potentiality of being a "political" band. But in the interim years we'd realized that denial is its own form of compliance and self-erasure. Plus, it's exhausting. We would go out on the road and play these songs and people could interpret them however the hell they wanted.

CHAPTER 17

OPENING UP

Some of the bands who opened for us went on to be huge: Yeah Yeah Yeahs, Gossip, the White Stripes, the Black Keys. No matter whether they would go on to blow up or break up or stay small, we wanted to tour with artists that we could stand to see night after night. Picking an opening band is an act of curation—you want there to be differentiation between the bands on the bill, but nothing too jarring, nothing that takes somebody out of the experience. And you don't want to be aggressively contrarian so that your audience isn't receptive to the openers, standing with crossed arms, counting down the minutes until you get onstage. It was always a very deliberate, considered decision for us. We wanted to expose our audience to new bands. Mostly, however, we wanted to feel challenged. We never wanted a band to play before us that wasn't capable of being a great live band, or that would make us seem bigger, louder, or tighter. We were confident enough to be matched, perhaps even usurped.

The Black Keys had just put out their first album when we asked them to come on the road with us for the second leg of the *One Beat* tour. Dan and Patrick were mournful and gritty onstage, affable and

Midwestern off; there was lots of pool playing. In Detroit, hometown
of the White Stripes, a particularly proud and loyal audience member,
with the intention of playing off a perceived rivalry, turned his back to
the Black Keys for the entirety of their set, his middle finger raised
defiantly in the air. You've got to appreciate a dedication analogous
to the crazed affection toward sports teams, but disrespect is another
matter altogether. Janet called the guy out during our show.

We brought the Gossip along with us on their first-ever tour, literally
the first time they'd played outside of Olympia. The first show was at
First Avenue in Minneapolis, a fairly large, well-established venue with
a particularly high stage. I recall watching singer Beth Ditto own that
stage within seconds of their set starting. They played exciting and
unrelenting blues music at the time, suggestive, dancey, unabashedly
Southern, queer, bold, and weird. Beth wasn't even twenty-one yet on
that tour. I drove them around Chicago, showed them the shores of
Lake Michigan; they crashed in our hotel rooms. I loved being witness
as they saw the United States for the first time, these three young
kids from Arkansas. They made us goofy and happy. We had dares
almost every night of the tour. They painted our faces with ridiculous
makeup—Janet was a marionette, I had freckles, Corin was a doll. We
lost bets and had to give embarrassing shoutouts involving crushes in
the middle of the set. At one point there was a conga line onstage. The
silliness was buoying, it staved off the tour tedium.

The White Stripes were the band that really pushed the limits of
what an opening band could do. You could still feel an electricity on
the stage and in the air once they were done. It was in 2000, just a few
months before they became one of the biggest bands around. It was the
first time we brought a support act wherein you could tell some people
in the audience were there just for them, that part of the audience didn't

give a shit about us even though we were headlining. But even then, even when the opening band was testing and trying us, we still had to play our set and prove that it shouldn't have been the reverse. (Later, when the White Stripes were huge, they asked us to open a few shows in order to repay the kindness and we gladly did. Jack White remains gracious, generous, and one of my favorite performers.) We always wanted to bring openers that raised our level of playing and performance; we were honored and excited to do it.

When the White Stripes were on tour with us, we played a show at Oberlin College in Ohio. The gig was in the student center, the kind of place where someone can order a slice of pizza only a few feet from stage and if you're not playing loud enough you might even hear the customer's name being called over the intercom. Backstage, Jack would entertain us with Loretta Lynn or Son House songs on guitar. He was a showman, always on, a peacock, but his prancing was never uninvited or unwanted. He always had a presence, a way of reaching the farthest corners of a room, that star quality of simultaneously sucking the air out of a space and giving it life. On this particular night we were confronted by the classic tour scenario: the promise of an after-party. It usually entails an intrepid kid approaching you and telling you about the event, how awesome it is going to be. He gives you his phone number or slips you an address on a piece of paper, which you often lose either on purpose or by accident. But this night we thought we'd give it a try. Often in small towns you feel slightly off the radar; this instills in you a sense of wildness and freedom, you feel inconspicuous, the vibe is casual. You're much more likely to end up hanging out with fans at a local bar in Lawrence, Kansas, or Omaha than in New York or L.A.

Corin was pregnant on this tour, so she wasn't always up for after-show revelry, or really for anything other than crashing out. So we rode with White Stripes to the address we were given. We walked up to the house and immediately two guys walked down the stairs and greeted us at the door. "Who are you?" they asked accusingly. They obviously hadn't been at our show. You'd think at Oberlin—a bastion of liberal arts education and hipness, a breeding ground for creative types spewing expression often for the sake of expression—that everyone would greet the bands that had just entertained their friends with open arms. We weren't expecting the keys to the city (okay, town), but at the very least we thought we could count on a knowing nod, a thumbs-up and all the free alcohol we wanted. This wasn't cotillion or prom or graduation that we were crashing—this was a party taking place in a wall-to-wall carpeted duplex with particleboard cabinets. Don't people want to hang with musicians? Yet band life is full of humbling moments such as these. It was an outright rejection. We were told that the party was full, as if there were a legal capacity to which they were adhering and only so many rubbery vegan hot dogs and red Solo cups to go around. I often think back on those two guys who turned us away, wondering if they know they kicked Jack White out of their party—if they saw him later on TV or in a magazine and thought he looked familiar, if he reminded them of the tall guy who stood helplessly on their front lawn and then walked back to an outdated, beat-up van. To me, it's the perfect distillation of the disparity between being onstage and being off. For all the power you command in a live context, all the myth and mythmaking that goes into that moment, elevated by the agreement between performer and audience, when you're offstage, you're shrunk down to human size, to the humility it takes to endure the quotidian.

In 2000, Greil Marcus named us the best rock band in America in *Time* magazine. The next morning on a talk show, Bryant Gumbel waved the magazine and asked incredulously, "Who is this band?"

It felt unreal. We'd never had a radio hit or sold any amount of albums nearing the status of gold or platinum. In the larger scheme of things—population-wise—hardly anyone had heard of us, least of all the subscribers of *Time*. We had taken the accompanying photos for the article while on tour; it all had to happen immediately, so they hastily set up a shoot all the way in Scotland. When we flew home a few weeks later, the magazine issue had just come out. Here we were, "America's Best Rock Band," unloading our equipment that had been shipped home from overseas, that we'd just picked up from the airport by ourselves: drums, amps, road cases. We did not even have the help of a friend or crewmember to carry everything out of our van and into Janet's basement, down rotted steps with very low headroom. You had to duck or you'd give yourself a concussion. "Best Band in America" and my back is about to go out again because I'm carrying a sixty-pound amp into a practice space the size of a pantry in which Janet's aged marmalade cat had sprayed multiple times. It smelled like piss and dryer sheets. This was us having "made it!" We never stopped working. Most bands don't.

There is very little about being a working musician that is glamorous, which is why I have never understood people who get onstage and hardly even try. What else is there besides that moment? Why would you waste it? In the '90s the term "slacker" was applied to a certain kind of breezy, laid-back male artist: Beck, Stephen Malkmus of Pavement, Rivers Cuomo of Weezer. These guys were understated, sneaker-wearing; they acted like they couldn't be bothered and had a tossed-off coolness. Lyrics seemed to pour out of their mouths in profound, poetic drips. They made it look casual, like the stakes were low or nonexistent. I admired and listened to the music, and I think the perception and reception were different from their intent. But I also thought about what a privilege it must be to feel—or to affect—that entitlement; to be on-stage, to play music, to get up in front of people and appear not to care.

Recently I saw a band play on *Saturday Night Live*. It's mostly one guy but he tours with 9+ people, all of them men. Every one of them wore T-shirts. If a group of nine women wore T-shirts on a national TV show, people would 1) ridicule them for not trying to look pretty, or 2) think it was an art project. At the very least it would be notable.

Though the term "slacker music" (not one that these musicians put upon themselves, I should stress) has since disappeared, certainly the affectlessness remains, the gutlessness, in many bands and artists that have come since. Entitlement is a precarious place from which to create or perform—it projects the idea that you have nothing to prove, noth-ing to claim, nothing to show but self-satisfaction, a smug boredom. It breeds ambivalence. It's as if instead of having to prove they are something, these musicians prove they aren't anything. It's an inverted dynamic, one that sets performers up to fail, but also gives them a false sense of having already arrived. I don't understand how someone would not push, challenge, or at least be present, how anyone could get onstage and not give *everything*.

Sleater-Kinney had to prove ourselves all over again when we re-turned to the opening slot in 2003. By then we'd become accustomed to headlining most of our own shows, but Pearl Jam invited us to join them on tour. Eddie Vedder had always been kind toward Sleater-Kinney. I met him at one of our shows in Seattle in 1998, outside the Crocodile Café. Eddie walked up and stood in line behind me and Corin. He introduced himself to us and said he felt like he was stand-ing next to Jagger and Richards. It's a compliment a girl doesn't hear too often.

When the invite came, we didn't hesitate. Bob Lawton knew that exposing our band to a bigger audience that would never know us otherwise was crucial. We felt like Pearl Jam was the right band to do that with. The financial offer was generous, the timing was right, and they were good people, like-minded Northwesterners.

Our first show with Pearl Jam was in Denver, on April Fools' Day. We'd been playing the fist-raising, call-to-arms songs off *One Beat* on our own tours in clubs and theaters around the world, but now we would perform in sports stadiums and arenas. Without giving it a second thought, Corin criticized George W. Bush from the stage. It was almost the first thing she said to a crowd of over fifteen thousand, at the Pepsi Center, people who had little or no idea who we were. To fans in the nosebleed section, we probably looked like ants, which was also how significant we were to most of these Pearl Jam listeners.

Calling out George W. for his warmongering was something our crowd would have practically expected from us. By April 2003, support for the dual wars in Iraq and Afghanistan was starting to dwindle, especially in the more left-leaning urban centers and cities. And one area where support for our then president was securely and almost universally out of favor was in the politically homogeneous indie rock and alternative music circles. Sleater-Kinney probably could have burned Bush in effigy or torn apart a life-size replica of him at the end of our sets and the crowds would have cheered, taking home destroyed doll remnants as souvenirs.

Pearl Jam, it turned out, played music to all kinds of people. Their fans were both rural and urban, Republicans and Democrats, and everything in between. The band was touring with their album *Riot Act*, which featured an excoriating song called "Bushleaguer." In Denver the song, or perhaps it was the George W. Bush rubber mask that Eddie pulled on, drew boos from the crowd. Yet five minutes later, that same sports-cap-wearing man with upper-arm hair and a cross around his neck who had booed Eddie would be tearing up, enacting a human seat belt on his eyelinered girlfriend and singing along to "Black." Here was the mainstream.

We had a lot to learn.

When you've only been on van tours—we wouldn't tour in a bus until *The Woods*—pulling up to a venue where professional sports teams play is humbling and intimidating. When we arrived to soundcheck in our fifteen-passenger Ford Econoline, it looked like we should be showing up to restock napkins at a concession stand or refill a vending machine. (And just at *one* stand or *one* machine, otherwise we would be driving a semi truck.) Everything around us was bigger and more formidable than our vehicle. The insignificance was acute.

Pearl Jam had multiple buses and semis, a private plane, a lighting rig, countless racks of gear, a mixing and monitor console, a separate recording facility and mixing board for documenting each show, a chef, a personal trainer, guitar and drum techs, and a general crew of over forty people.

Our three-person crew would load our two amps and one drum kit onto a stage the size of the entire venues we'd been playing up until that point. We set up our gear in front of a wall of beautiful vintage amps, high-tech gear, drum and piano risers. Each member of Pearl Jam came with not simply his own equipment but his own section, his own *world*. From up there on the stage it resembled consecutive dorm rooms, each guy's area affixed with personal touches and mementos. It was exciting and grand, larger than life.

———

Though I had no reservations about touring with Pearl Jam, elitism was a stubborn habit to kick. A small part of my brain retreated to my younger self, reminding me that in certain circles Nirvana had been considered the *cooler*, more authentic band. Nirvana's music dragged you across the floor, you felt every crack, every speck of dirt. Their songs helped you locate the places where you ached, and in that awareness of your hurting you suddenly knew that the bleakness was collective, not merely your own. In other words, it's okay to feel like a freak. And in high school, and for much of my adult life, maybe even now, I had, I do.

So, I'll be honest, I wondered whether I could like Pearl Jam's music, not just the hits I knew might stoke my high school nostalgia, but the entirety of the band, their sound, their thing. Their songs had solos— multiple solos! They had ballads to take the room down a bit and anthems to bring the room back up; they possessed a mastery in a genre in which I had become accustomed to scoffing at mastery as an automatic equivalent to or indication of quality. Also, they seemed *normal*. And bubbling up from the formative years that shaped my relationship to outsider art, which I loved and related to, I still held on to my skepticism of normality. The greater mental hurdle was whether we wanted to—or were capable of—playing in front of the Pearl Jam audience. For as sweet as those guys were, their audience felt alien. It was mainstream, for one, and perhaps not ready or willing to make sense of three women making a racket, with no bass, very few solos, and an angularity not easily digestible. But we felt it was an opportunity we shouldn't pass up; it would be a challenge, and we had not been an opening band for a long time.

Any leftover snobbery about Pearl Jam changed after the first show.

No matter how much crew a band or musician takes on tour, whether they travel in relative luxury or squalor, whether someone else tunes their guitar for them or switches pedal settings from the side of the stage, the bottom line is, at some point, it's just people onstage playing music, doing a job. And for the best of these performers, among whom I count Eddie Vedder, there is no holding back, no wasted moment.

What I discovered was that Pearl Jam's music was soaring. Vedder's lyrics spoke to pain and anger but offered a way out; there was a hopefulness to them, they came from a singer who wanted to live, to be alive. By the end of the tour, Sleater-Kinney was joining Pearl Jam onstage for the encore, singing and playing along to Neil Young's "Rockin' in the Free World" and "Harvest Moon." The band shared the experience, made it about us and about their fans.

Vedder felt a true kinship with me and with my band. He was a punk and agitator who had ended up in one of the world's most popular groups. And each night he managed to relay tremendous generosity and openness. At the end of the first and longest tour we would do with them, he gave me his custom Gibson SG Special. I play it to this day.

I love being a new onlooker, a convert. To become a fan of something, to open and change, is a move of deliberate optimism, curiosity, and enthusiasm. Touring with Pearl Jam allowed me to see how diminishing and stifling it is to close yourself off to experiences. It was a tour that changed my life.

It turns out that if we hadn't toured with Pearl Jam, we probably would not have made *The Woods*. We walked onstage each night with the stakes high, which is a hard place to return to for a band that's been around for nearly a decade. But we were unknown here—we felt brand-new, untested, unloved. It forced us to turn inward, to focus on why we played and how we played. We had to listen to one another, to count on one another as the source of joy and givers of the only rewards. We had to find intrinsic value in what we were doing, to not rely on the audience to compensate for any of our own lack of energy or drive or desire. And certainly there were Pearl Jam fans who liked us, who walked back from getting their hot dogs and beer and who eventually looked up from their conversations to watch a song or two.

I waited for those moments each night. The daylight was fading, it felt like the real concert was happening *after* us, but we had to make it real each night, to bring to what was so clearly not the main event an intensity that would raise the audience's eyes to us. Without the help of lights or cheers, we inserted ourselves into the landscape. And a few people took notice. By the time we finished, there would be people standing, watching, listening. Since few of them knew our songs, we had no one to please, and we started jamming at the end of the sets, just for ourselves, partly to get people's attention, to make something so long and drawn-out as to foment discomfort, to defy expectations, and partly to surprise ourselves as much as them, to keep it interesting for us. And in deconstructing our own songs, we found that we were building something anew: a trust in what we were as a band and what we could still become.

CHAPTER 18

THE WOODS

Opening for Pearl Jam enabled and emboldened us, and it instilled in us a desire to write songs that had improvisational moments built in. So on *The Woods* there are moments that break apart, disintegrate, allow the opportunity to rebuild. Instead of approaching a song as something small, we started big, and we carved smallness and detail out of a broader canvas. I don't know if we could have envisioned that broadness if we hadn't played on a big stage, heard our sound echo around an amphitheater. And that's how we got from *One Beat* to *The Woods*. It's what made us a better live band and reminded us that it could feel uncertain, and that sense of uncertainty was how we were going to create something better.

Sleater-Kinney was nearing the decade mark of being a band. It felt like we knew our capabilities, that they were approaching something finite and fixed. And our audience knew what we were capable of, what we were going to sound like, who our label was; the people who didn't like us would continue to not like us, and the people who liked us would feel the same, ad infinitum. I could imagine that the journalists had already written their reviews, like the obituaries on deck for the nearly dead; someone could just plug in the name of our latest album and the review would be done. I didn't want to be the Mr. Rogers of music, where we could open a closet and see the same ten sweaters, and everyone would know what we were going to wear since there was a predetermined set of choices. None of us were that excited about that anymore. I don't want to know what's going to happen. As frightening as that is in real life, it's a crucial aspect in creativity. Being predictable is boring, and it's also disheartening and uninspiring. We needed a sense of rediscovery, for the audience and for ourselves.

We had always recorded in Portland or Seattle, places that were or felt like home, and we'd recorded with someone we'd known for years, who was part of our community; we were still working with the label we had worked with basically from the beginning. With *The Woods*, we pulled the rug out from underneath ourselves, a potentially self-sabotaging risk. But changes had also happened unwittingly—we were already one foot out the door, dangling. Bob Lawton, our longtime booking agent and one of our most consistent and loyal team members, decided to retire. And Julie Butterfield, who had been our PR person, our manager, a source of reason and guidance, and a close friend throughout all of the band's history, had also decided to embark on something different. Two of our pillars were knocked out already. So, when we thought about Kill Rock Stars, our label and a group of people we loved, we realized that maybe we should take *all* the known factors and comforts away and start over as much as we could.

You can't really be reborn, but we wanted to create an ersatz beginning. We started looking for a new label and landed with Sub Pop; we got a new booking agent; we hired a producer we'd never worked with before; we cobbled together a whole new existence for ourselves. From a songwriting perspective, it was invigorating, but on a personal level, it was stressful for each of us.

Our songwriting process had changed. For a while I thought academia was pulling me in a different direction from the band, and in the fall of 2003, I moved to Berkeley for a relationship and to test out the potential of attending graduate school. Ever since those early days of Sleater-Kinney playing shows at Bryn Mawr or Wesleyan, I'd imagined a different kind of life for myself, a quieter life, one I thought to have more consistency and normalcy. Yet here I was, practicing a more domestic self in a sunny Berkeley bungalow, and I felt fitful and dissatisfied. I applied to two low-residency MFA programs in nonfiction and was accepted to both, but as I spent time around academics in the Bay Area, my desire to be in that world faded. With music, I had been working in a populist medium, whereas academia felt insular and impenetrable. I wanted my work to be found, discovered, available. And I was fooling myself thinking that I could or would give up the one thing, music, that, although peripatetic and jolting and full of vicissitudes, had also brought me the most joy, the most highs, the most connection I had ever felt.

Over those six months in California, with Portland in the rearview mirror and the band something I could examine with some distance, I realized my yearning had little to do with place and more with the fact that I continually made a ritual of emptiness. No matter where I was or what I was doing, I would always feel a certain deficit. Like before, as a way to fill the hole, I began writing songs. Music began to restore me again.

Living in California informed many of my lyrics on *The Woods*. While there, I read a Tad Friend article in *The New Yorker* about suicides on the Golden Gate Bridge. I wrote the song "Jumpers" about this piece. I read it as I was taking BART into the city, and I found myself crying and thinking about how out of place I felt. I had never lived outside the Pacific Northwest before. And I couldn't understand why, in this place of such intense beauty and sun—and where I assumed I'd find those things invigorating—I felt a sharp, alienating contrast. I related to the feeling of not being able to find meaning in your life, so that you try to find a way of instilling meaning in your death, looking for a way for it to somehow be symbolic or beautiful or publicly acknowledged. The Golden Gate Bridge is a structure that is extraordinarily solid in terms of engineering prowess, but unstable in that it's a launching place for those in despair. I wanted to write about the instability of structures, whether they're internal structures that we thought were holding us together or political structures that we thought were stable or safe, that we could rely on for doing good. I felt a weakening in the foundation; I guess I didn't know that foundation might be the band itself, that things I thought I could count on were starting to dismantle.

I returned to Portland and the band with an almost desperate relief. I bought the house I still live in, latching on to my own small square of the city with a sense of new permanence. Janet and Corin and I could once again write on a regular basis instead of on my limited bimonthly commutes. Writing for *The Woods* marked another shift. Less often did Corin or I bring in parts of a song or an entire song. Now Janet and I were doing a lot more of the songwriting, while Corin was busy with family. We had to push her, and she was reluctant to be pushed. Sleater-Kinney were making our scariest record, and Corin was a mother with a young kid; it was natural that in that realm—in parenthood—she wanted to ward off and protect her kin from horrors, to bring light and happiness into her world. Yet Janet and I were really embracing harshness and leaning into something sonically and thematically dark. We felt there was a creeping tepidness in music, a cloying softness, as if music were only a salve, not an instigator. It's not that we didn't listen

to or appreciate pretty songs, or that music couldn't merely be for entertainment. I can listen to soft songs, but I can't play them. Even Sleater-
Kinney's lighter songs feel thorny or brittle—they aren't gentle, and
they make horrible background music. Janet and I wanted this record
to have teeth. Corin didn't quite feel the same intensity at this point.
There was tension.

When Corin finally got there, especially vocally, she went *way* out
there—but I feel like we shoved her. On the chorus of "Let's Call It
Love," she sounds mad and desperate, longing and lost—we tossed her
out into the ether and you can hear her singing her way back; the notes
are carrying her, but it's not pretty. It's the sound of someone fighting
against herself and against her doubters, who in that moment happened to be in her own band. I think *The Woods* turned out exactly how
we wanted it, but the process was very painful.

Janet was the one who found and reached out to Dave Fridmann. At
the time he was mainly known for his work with the Flaming Lips.
Dave only works in one studio, which is in Cassadaga, New York. Ini-
tially, we thought it sounded glamorous to record in New York, and I
imagined weekend trips to the city. In actuality, Cassadaga is tucked
away in the far western part of the state, near Buffalo, more than eight
hours from New York City. Plus, we were recording in the depths of
winter and were snowed in most of the time. We stayed at the house
attached to the recording studio, where we felt isolated, entrenched in a
wholly immersive and insular experience. We didn't have the luxury, at
the end of the day, of returning to our regular world, to our friends and
relationships and animals and families. The intensity never let up: we
ate and slept and breathed the music. While one of us was cooking, the
others would continue working, then we'd all eat together. After a full

day of recording, we'd go up to our rooms and watch movies or TV shows until four a.m. We watched music documentaries and burned through *Freaks and Geeks*. We played Led Zeppelin records and read. We were too wired and rarely slept.

In the mornings we'd take walks in the woods with sticks to protect ourselves from the undersocialized, overly protective country dogs, and we'd wear orange vests on account of hunting season. Then it would snow again and we would sled down the hill, careening and careless, mostly ending up in ditches. The neighbor boys came over and let us fire their shotguns at bottles, or took us out on their ATVs; it felt like good, clean fun, in such contrast to what we were unleashing in the studio, which felt raw and messy.

Dave told us to let him produce and have a say on this record, or we shouldn't work with him at all. It was a scary prospect. We were accustomed to having total control; John Goodmanson was always wary of overstepping, of intruding too heavily on our process. But we were willing. When we first arrived in Cassadaga, Dave sat in the room with a notepad while we played the songs for him. He would question why a certain song part needed to be there, and we either had to justify the structure or reasoning, or change it. It was an intimidating but important process. On "What's Mine Is Yours," which abruptly changes in the middle of the song, it was Dave's idea to have it completely fall apart. Originally the song went from the second chorus into a bridge, but his thought was that if we wanted a change, it should be noticeable. He said, "Why doesn't everyone just stop playing and see what happens?" And that's how we got a sudden long weird guitar solo in the middle of the song—one of us had to come in, otherwise there was just silence, so I played until everyone else found their way back into the song. Fridmann created a lot of ledges for us to jump off. His way of describing what he wanted to hear was very visual and textural. He told Janet, "I need you to sound like Keith Moon, but like I'm lowering a blanket over Keith Moon." We trusted him right away, and when we heard ourselves back after the first takes, we knew we had found the right person.

I suppose many of our longtime listeners were upset because we were taking perfectly normal songs and making them hard to listen to; the sound was blown out and grating. We wanted to make something fractious; we didn't want to please or appease. Perhaps that sounds arrogant or even callous, but we recoiled at the common, tacit expectation that the more records you make, the more they'll start to feel cozy, settled in, mellowed out. Daddy rock, mommy rock, lullabies, as if once we're no longer in our twenties we're just supposed to soothe ourselves to sleep every night. We were more prone to insomnia, at our most awake in the dark.

The very first show for *The Woods* tour felt inauspicious. We played the Moore Theatre in Seattle. I wore a typically bizarre polyester shirt with a large bow, buttoned too tight and high up on the neck to be conducive to performing. (That "business casual" vibe is hard to quit.) It was another one of those sartorial choices—like a cowboy hat or faux-fur jacket—to be categorized in the "bad tour purchase" column. After the show, we were backstage celebrating with Sub Pop, whose employees had all come to the show in their hometown. I could feel my neck getting hot.

At first I thought it was the shirt. But then came the familiar feeling of my ears swelling and closing. I was breaking out in hives. My breathing grew tight. I left the festivities. My dad and a friend of mine took me to the emergency room, where I stayed until nearly four a.m., amped up on steroids for the swelling, which were in direct competition with the Benadryl I had taken prior. I woke up in my father's guest room, groggy, with puffy eyes. We had a show to play in Portland that night.

Our big hometown show to debut the new record was at the Crystal Ballroom, a large venue downtown. A few minutes before I had to head to soundcheck, I walked into my bathroom and looked at myself in the mirror. My eyes were still swollen from the allergic reaction the night before; the hives had diminished but my skin looked mottled. My face was its own Halloween mask. Then I couldn't breathe. I was outside myself looking in, I was on the wall of the bathroom, I was outside my house, a satellite. I could feel my smallness. When my chest constricted, it was not on account of my rib cage but of the universe enveloping me and folding me into its vastness, its nothingness. I called Corin to tell her that I was having chest pains and that I'd be missing soundcheck. I drove myself to a hospital in northwest Portland. They hooked me up to an EKG machine, which of course determined that I wasn't having a heart attack, that physically I was fine—it only proved that perhaps my brain wasn't. It was a panic attack, possibly exacerbated by the steroids, which I'd need to stay on for a few more days.

My body wanted me to take it easy, but in some ways we were already taking it incredibly easy. After Corin had her son, Marshall, our touring became less intense. Her responsibility to Marshall and her desire to spend more time at home and less time on the road reshaped our schedule. The first leg of the tour for *The Woods* would only be a month long. We took care of ourselves: we didn't smoke or do any drugs—we barely drank. We did do a lot of the work by ourselves. We still helped load our own gear, designed our own T-shirts, consulted on and approved PR and marketing strategies. But this tour we'd get to take a bus, so for the first time we wouldn't literally be driving ourselves to the shows. I'm not complaining. A band is a small business, and we liked being hands-on, part of the decision-making process; we liked being in control.

Corin with her sleepy infant son, Marshall. During the writing of One Beat. *Portland.*

It's no wonder that many artists deal with tour by desensitizing themselves until the moment they are onstage. Tour is a precarious nexus between monotony and monomania—a day of nothingness followed by a moment that feels like everything. You deal with tour by reading, walking, watching TV or movies, zoning out online. If you're lucky, you engage in an activity that posits you in a specific place: a museum, a visit with a friend, a local restaurant. But most of the day feels shapeless, a blurriness that comes into focus only once you soundcheck and begin the progression toward the show itself. Even the day's most mundane activities—eating, drinking coffee, working out in the hotel gym, doing a phone interview with a weekly paper for an upcoming show—all of these things carry with them a sense of validation and productivity because they are couched within the sphere of tour. But in actuality, it is aimless. If it's not already numbing, you find a way to get numb.

Even missing someone or something is dangerous, because it takes you out of tour. When I moved back to Portland to write *The Woods*, I wanted to find a way of tethering myself to a place, to home, and so I adopted a dog. Up until that point I had few domestic responsibilities, save for my two cats, that I could take on or be competent in. If you're in a band, you're surrounded by few demarcations of maturity in the traditional sense, because you're perennially enacting fairly adolescent behavior. It's an unconventional life. Of course, some people get married and have children, but just as many people in that world don't. A music career, especially for a woman, is so at odds with the assumed normative path toward maturity and aging.

Tobey was a wirehaired pointer mix with a challenging combination of intelligence and wild energy. At first I was obsessive: this was a whole new skill set to learn. I dove into training, research, problem-solving. Tobey provided a certain level of distraction that I really liked. He was impossible and stubborn and adorable. Janet got a dog, too, and we would take them on the short legs of tours. I loved the sense of companionship, though I had moments of panic, too—this was something I really had to commit to, this dog. Leaving Tobey made it harder to tour because he became a reminder of how much I was away.

The rest of the U.S. tour I made it through without medical incident. Our final show was in Denver. We were playing the last song of the regular set, "Entertain," when my palms began to itch. This was not a mild sensation but an incessant, unignorable nuisance—I would scratch furiously and then strum at my guitar. The itchiness was a bizarre intrusion of bodily reality into an experience that usually obliviates the quotidian. By then, "Entertain" was a song that we elongated with an improvised jam, stretching out our enjoyment of the set and of the crowd. But on this night I couldn't think of anything other than the hives. I could tell one of my eyes was swelling shut and I mouthed to Corin, "Allergic reaction." We abruptly finished the song and our tour manager drove me to the nearest hospital.

The reaction was ten times worse than it had been in Seattle. The doctors gave me two shots of adrenaline to prevent me from going into anaphylactic shock. Both eyes swelled shut. Instead of toasting to a successful tour and hanging out with our crew, Janet and Corin drove to the hospital. We spent the last night of tour sitting around my hospital bed.

When I got home, I saw a specialist who determined that I had a food allergy. Looking back, I realized that each incident of hives had been preceded by the consumption of soy. The doctor called it "exercise-induced anaphylaxis." Instead of having a normal reaction, the sweat and increased heart rate expedites the speed with which the allergen courses through the body, making it potentially life-threatening.

But also, allergies? Hives? These are not the afflictions of rock bands or guitarists. "Hives" doesn't really have the same ring to it as, say, "heroin," and it falls far short of legendary potential. Nor are there any memorable songs about allergies, at least none sung for adults. With allergies you don't get to venture into the euphemism "exhaustion" like you do if you lose your mind, throw a fit, punch someone in the face, go on a racist social media rant, or get arrested. Nope, I was sane, high-functioning, a little on the anxious and depressive side, and now saddled with an affliction that would garner me more sympathy at a natural grocer or with the PTA than with music journalists or fans. Not necessarily fodder for *Behind the Music*.

Next up to promote *The Woods* was a European tour that would begin in the UK. England in particular had long been fairly indifferent toward Sleater-Kinney, but for some reason they were enamored of *The Woods*. The British press love when American bands play at Americanness (the same way the U.S. eats up the Brits playing at being Brits). It is a satisfying cycle of self-validation, a country imagined by outsiders. And I suppose *The Woods* was our own scrappy version of a national anthem of a frontier, jagged and belted through a crackling megaphone. We were excited to finally be met with more than just a mild enthusiasm overseas. Our first show was at All Tomorrow's Parties, a weekend festival we co-curated with the Shins and Dinosaur Jr.

Two days before we flew out, I felt a sharp pain in my side. The more hypochondriacal part of me momentarily feared appendicitis. But I chalked it up to the typical pre-tour anxiety and set forth with all of the enthusiasm and eagerness I could muster.

ATP is held in the south of England at a resort called Pontins. The American equivalent of this facility would be like staying at a Super 8 motel still decorated for Easter three months past the holiday and featuring a rain-soaked outdated McDonald's play area partially closed for construction. Here, the pain in my side bloomed into a small rash. Yet much of tour is about ignoring the body instead of listening to it, so we continued on to France. By now, instead of the rash spreading or dissipating, it had become a series of perfectly round blisters. They were painful but the surface area they covered was small. I convinced myself that it was from my guitar, the combined result of sweat and chafing, even though nothing of the sort had ever previously occurred. In addition—and to feel like I was being proactive—I purchased a cream at a pharmacy, since cream seemed like the least intrusive and most readily available solution. On we went to Germany.

By now I was walking around in a state of anxiety. I would fall in and out of panic attacks; the feeling of breathlessness and choking was intermittent, bordering on constant. More disconcerting was the feeling of unreality, similar to what I'd experienced in the bathroom mirror before the show in Portland at the beginning of the *Woods* tour. I felt separate from my body, a tingling in my limbs like a slow vanishing.

After our show in Berlin, with the symptoms and the unease now impossible to ignore, Janet and I took a taxi to a hospital in the eastern part of the city. We arrived at a series of austere, windowless structures. They had an eerie architectural sternness, a building crossing its arms. In the waiting room a young man sat with a bloody urine sample in his lap. The act of sitting, of waiting—despite being in a foreign country, despite not even really knowing what was wrong with me—was strangely familiar and comforting. This was consistency. Being sick had become my remedy for tour.

Finally I was escorted down a dimly lit hallway to a small room with an impossibly high exam table. I sat in an adjoining chair and waited. A doctor came in and looked at my stomach. He spoke very little English and I spoke no German. He left the room and returned with a book. He opened to a page with a series of pictures. I felt like he was a tourist trying to order at a restaurant, using one of those pictorial guide books that allow you to have little grasp of the language but to nevertheless explain your needs by pointing at what you want. What this doctor wanted was to show me what exactly was ailing me. So he pointed at a close-up photograph of a rash that looked like mine. Written below the photo was the word, first in German, but then in an array of letters that I understood: *shingles*.

He gave me a prescription for anti-viral meds and pain pills and I was off into the night. We stopped at a 24-hour pharmacy and went back to the hotel.

The next morning we met in the lobby to set off for our next shows. Embarrassed, I let the crew know about the shingles. There was talk about whether to cancel the tour, but I was convinced that we shouldn't. There were only about two more weeks left.

Shingles, in case you're under the age of sixty-five or have never been ridden with stress-induced illness, is a reoccurrence of the chickenpox virus, which lies dormant in your body. Painful blisters form along nerve endings, usually only manifesting themselves on one side of the body. Shingles is quite contagious, especially before the blisters have fully scabbed over, though you can't give someone shingles. You can, however, give chickenpox to someone who has never had it. And what I swiftly found out was that Janet had never had chickenpox.

I felt like a walking infection, zombiefied and pestiferous. Tour's insularity can be what makes it wonderful and magical and sort of like summer camp. But that same insularity coupled with an infectious illness is more a horror film. If we could have found humor in the situation, it would have made for an amazing parody, but there was very little laughter at this point. We were driving around Europe in our van, with a limited amount of air circulating through a cramped space. I was very conscious of trying not to expose Janet to the shingles, and she obviously didn't want to be anywhere near me. I kept my headphones on and stared at my computer. More than the virus, a sense of disappointment filled the air.

By the time we'd reached Brussels, my body felt like a bag my brain was carrying with me: heavy, the weight unevenly distributed, the contents mashed and scrambled. I felt raw and scraped, like a human crayon, dragging myself across surfaces, leaving a foamy smudge.

The show in Brussels was at Le Botanique, a greenhouse-like structure, glass and octagonal, with an abundant echo both of history and of the voices and footsteps of the present day. It was grand, superb. I was a sick speck.

Janet was on the phone with one of her sisters, a doctor, who explained the airborne nature of shingles. I was contagious, unleashed and on the loose. I felt nothing but exhaustion, guilt, and shame. That's when Corin helped me with my shirt; she was delicate on account of my own discomfort but also hers. Here she was mothering me, missing her own kid back at home. This could hardly be worth it, I thought, for her, for me.

It was time for us to play, but I for once couldn't access any reserves. I felt like mush, murky. I was an outsider and outside, undone and unraveled. I started to cry. It was that ugly kind of sadness, of wailing, where your face distorts, lips curl, your features cascade like a waterfall. And then . . .

WHACK.

I punched myself in the face.

Over and over. I repeated the motion. Each blow brought the feeling to the surface. The hatred rose up and I hit it back down. I saw the enemy and it was me; I wanted to destroy it. *Pow!* I couldn't stop. *Thud!* You fucking fraud. I was in the ring with only myself. Here's your fear. *Punch.* Here's your anger. Here's every sickness you've ever known. *Slap.* Here's your powerlessness. *Smack!*

I boxed myself to oblivion.

I was going to make myself extinct.

———

Janet and Corin were standing in front of me now. They were yelling at me to stop and they were horrified. I knew that. I could sense their pity, fear, resignation. My hands were their voices and their judgment, their disappointment, but mostly my own. I was a child throwing a tantrum. But I wasn't an infant. I was thirty-two years old and one-third of a band that relied on me every single day and night, one-third of a partnership wherein the other two people depended on me for their livelihood. Each hit was the end. The end. We were past the end.

In a matter of minutes Sleater-Kinney was gone. I had knocked its lights out. TKO.

We would play the next show from this fresh grave.

My face was hot and stinging. My skin felt loose, like it was sliding off my skull. We still had to perform. Nearly forty-five minutes late, we walked onto the stage, not looking at one another, our Belgian promoter stupefied but polite. I played the whole set looking down, feeling like an outline of myself, trying to make my shape familiar to the audience, to the onlookers, since I had no sense of my body at all. I didn't talk, smile, look; staying put was all I had. Halfway through the set I realized that no one could tell. That the difference between half-dead and distraught and fully living could potentially go undetected. And that's when I knew I wanted to stop. I was done. I had dragged Sleater-Kinney into oblivion, a place we used to get to with our music. I took us there with hurt.

—————

When we walked offstage and returned to the dressing room, everything had changed. Colors and shapes, nothing was the same; it was a planetary shift, a foreign sphere that only hours before had signified total familiarity. I knew right then and there that the band was done. Corin wanted my father to come get me. But we kept going. We had another week or so of shows. The tension was palpable, the nights were joyless. No one trusted me. The band gave me my own hotel room so that I could sleep; I would lie in bed at night and talk to my dad. With the time difference he was at his office. It was the same feeling I had of swimming with him as a child—I clung to him. But I felt misshapen, lost. I couldn't locate myself on any map, in anyone's world, least of all my own.

Tour ended. We flew home and planned our last shows. We wrote a brief letter to the fans that we put on our website. We called what we were about to embark on a hiatus, as if it were a painless, bloodless pause.

We have not talked about that night in Brussels since.

CHAPTER 19

BE STILL THIS SAD YEAR

When we returned from tour, we all felt broken. Each of us had something that wasn't working anymore. The only reason we had kept doing Sleater-Kinney year after year was because the rewards outweighed the amount of work and the difficulties, the heartbreak and the frustrations. But we had reached a point where the cracks couldn't easily be filled, assuaged, or mitigated by a great live show. The damage felt transparent. The larger truth was that Corin was also tired of touring, conflicted about leaving her family, feeling a disconnect between wanting to provide comfort to a child while sitting in the constant discomfort of a musician's life. I started seeing a psychiatrist who put me on medication for anxiety and depression. I apologized, I tried to make amends with the band. After the shame of what I'd done came a kind of relief. Janet and Corin and I reached something close to peaceable for the remaining tour dates. We tried to view them as celebratory.

We'd always come home from tours exhausted. We'd had fights during the *Dig Me Out* and *Hot Rock* tours that were immense compared to any squabbles we'd had since. We'd been a band for ten years. With *The Woods*, I felt that we had accomplished a great deal, pushed ourselves as far as we could go at that point. We had succeeded in redefining our own identity, our own music, reigniting the imaginations of music fans and what people thought we were. It would have been difficult to continue on without a struggle; it seemed like the journey had run its course. We ended the band at the best time we could, when people really wanted us to stay.

If we had been more calculated or had stronger management, maybe we would have strategized the end differently, made an announcement, put a final tour on sale, so everyone who wanted to could come and see us one last time. But that wasn't really the way that it was. Nothing felt celebratory; we didn't want to run a victory lap, especially since it felt like we'd left the race prematurely. Certainly someone with more business acumen might have been able to capitalize on the end of Sleater-Kinney. Instead, we had some East Coast shows already booked as warm-ups for Lollapalooza. When we made the announcement on our website about the impending indefinite hiatus, those shows suddenly carried more weight and meaning.

The final show in New York, at Webster Hall, was not our best. We had hired a film crew thinking we should capture some of these performances, maybe put out a DVD. By now we felt very confident in our live show, nimble, commanding, powerful. For *The Woods* tours, we had brought along the lighting director Stan Elleflot. He has a long shock of white hair, dreadlocks forming sporadically: part Scandinavian hipster, part drifter. Very gentle. Like any good LD, he helped the audience hear the music through visuals. Yet for some reason, we let the film crew dictate the lights for the Webster Hall show. They claimed that they needed the lighting to be very bright, very static. It was lit like a dressing room in a department store, everything was *on*. My hair shrank from the moisture alone, I could feel it getting smaller and smaller, tighter on my head. Meanwhile, my shirt was completely soaked through. I could barely play from the sweat dripping down my arms and hands. It was turning into a completely aquatic experience. Even during the performance I was aware of how awful this footage would look, and that we should never put out the DVD unless we included a sticker on the cover that said something to the effect of: "Hey, the three ugliest women in America have been in a band for the past ten years, have you seen them?"

Here we were playing a city that had always been generous and welcoming to us, one we looked up to, aspired and strived to deserve and impress. But we turned Webster Hall into a veritable tanning salon. The footage was entirely unusable. Like many aspects of our career, it *nearly* worked. It almost succeeded. That could be our band biography. *Almost*, by Sleater-Kinney.

Then in D.C. a heat wave hit. At the 9:30 Club the generator went out: no power, no air-conditioning. Fans had driven from all along the Eastern Seaboard, as far away as Florida, for this gig, taken days off work. Panic and stress set in. Even if we rescheduled the show in a few days, would these people be able to come back? We ended up flying to Chicago, playing Lollapalooza, and then returning to D.C. Each show started to feel like a countdown. We would start playing the songs, especially ones like "Call the Doctor" or "Little Babies," tunes we'd been playing for over nine years, and I would realize that this might be one of the last times I ever played these songs. The feeling was heavy, but I didn't want to think about how it might be perceived from the outside. It seemed crucial to stay in the moment, to feel our way through those last shows, to enjoy them.

Except for scheduling a final show in Portland, we didn't formalize a way for fans to say good-bye. We wanted to go out in a way that acknowledged our history, and that was also respectful to ourselves and to the fans. But we didn't want to feel like a museum piece, to apply some kind of unnecessary or self-aggrandizing gravity to the situation. We were a band. We were here, and then we weren't.

In August we played our final two shows—we added a second when the first instantly sold out—in Portland. Tickets were twelve dollars, our typical price. People traveled from around the world to see us out. It was flattering and bittersweet.

We rehearsed for our last two shows in a minuscule practice space inside a facility shared with countless other Portland bands. Windowless, with dirty, blotted walls, our amps set up facing one another, the drums within arm's reach; we were a cluster, a huddle. You start in a tiny room and you end in one, too. Just me and Corin and Janet and a decade of songs between us. We had played those songs for thousands upon thousands of people, but now, as at the beginning, we would play them for only each other.

We ran through the proposed set list. We would draw from the entirety of the catalog, which was common for our live show, though we often favored the most current album. This time, however, we wanted to highlight our favorites, the songs dearest to us, the ones to which our fans felt closest. The only moment that acknowledged the weight of the situation was when we played "Jumpers," the song about suicides on the Golden Gate Bridge, a song I had written during a bout of depression. The middle section of the song goes like this:

Be still this old heart
Be still this old skin
Drink your last drink
Sin your last sin
Sing your last song
About the beginning
Sing it out loud
So the people can hear
Be still this sad day
Be still this sad year
Hope your last hope
Fear your last fear

I could barely get the words out. When we finished the song, Corin and I were both crying. It's when and how I said my own good-bye.

August 12, 2006. The backstage at the Crystal Ballroom, a historic Portland venue where the band had played some of our biggest and best hometown shows, was both celebratory and funereal. There were flowers and champagne, friends and family. We took pictures and warmed up, stretched and dressed, conferred on the set list, visited with old friends, caught a few minutes of the opening acts we'd asked to play. Our moms and dads and siblings wore our concert T-shirts from throughout the years. It was a dizzying, glorious parade but also like watching someone put your life behind museum glass; you could feel the air being sucked out of the room, of the band, of your body.

The second-to-last show had an incredible crowd. It was the biggest mosh pit I had seen in years: the whole floor was moving, vibrating as a single organism. For the final show, Eddie Vedder came down from Seattle to give us a send-off. One of the most caring and soulful people I've ever met, he took the stage before we did, just like he had on all those nights we opened up for Pearl Jam. He stood up there in front of our crowd this time, ukulele in hand, and said that he'd always wished he had been able to see the Beatles or Led Zeppelin in their prime, or Keith Moon play with the Who, but that he felt lucky to have seen Sleater-Kinney. In one sentence he summed up for me what so many critics and pundits missed every time they put modifiers on our music, on our identity as a band. All we ever wanted was just to play songs and shows that mattered to people, that mattered to us. Music that summed up the messiness of life, that mitigated that nagging fear of hopelessness, loneliness, and death. That night, we played for a roomful of the people who understood that very thing. Once again, I felt privileged, lucky.

That final show was more contemplative, slightly maudlin. There was a lot of pressure on the two performances, for them to somehow—impossibly—be the summation of our entire career as a band. But there was so much about Sleater-Kinney, about the three of us, that was never sung or said or played at those final performances. I mentioned from the stage that this band had saved my life over and over again, and I think that is true. When we finished the show, there wasn't any real closure; it just felt like it always does, the three of us trying to pass something on to the crowd, hoping it was good enough.

PART 3
AFTERMATH

CHAPTER 20

SHELTER

With Tobey at my father's house in central Washington.

People always ask me if I was sad when Sleater-Kinney broke up. Mostly I felt a sense of relief. My grief was on hold, my emotions compartmentalized and transferred. The band was a phantom limb: I could still feel it there, I didn't really believe that it was gone, but mostly I ignored it. In a small room on the second floor of my house, a former attic built out by the previous owners, with slanted ceilings and corners only accessible by crawling, I placed a striped wool rug, a guitar, and a lone amplifier.

The only time I entered the room was to pet my cat Hector, who often sat in there atop a carpeted "cat condo" and watched over the contents of the space like a furry museum guard.

Instead of playing or thinking about music, I dove into my volunteer work at the Oregon Humane Society, which is just about the only way I knew how to deal with the loss. If you're wondering how sad I was, you'd never know by talking to me, but you would know it by the fact that I won the Oregon Humane Society Volunteer of the Year Award in 2006, the year of Sleater-Kinney's demise.

I clocked in over one hundred hours that year. I developed new programs to help long-term canine shelter residents get adopted, I made laminated flyers replete with photos I took of the dogs and added pat, inspirational, and euphemistic phrases like "If you love a toothy kiss, you'll love Buster" to promote specific dogs. I walked them on the shelter grounds and even took them on field trips. I taught the more rambunctious dogs to sit, wait, go to their bed, how to walk better on the leash. I sat in the lobby wearing my teal volunteer apron with two large front pockets gritty with dog treat remnants, torn and gooey from overeager puppy mouths, stretched from too much wear and not enough washing. I greeted customers in the lobby, grateful to be in a uniform, just one of many, anonymous and near invisible in a place where frumpiness and depression thrive. The dogs I brought with me to the lobby were my interlocutors, my translators; they bounded up to customers and I channeled their optimism. They lived in the moment, grateful for the interaction, and so was I. I had a purpose, even if part of that purpose was hosing down feces-covered kennels. The dogs' needs seemed simple, and I required simple needs: to have somewhere to be. It's easy to feel sated when all you're asking for in life is food, water, and some gentle petting.

I befriended the older women who made up the majority of the other volunteers. Retirees and former powerhouses in realms like consulting and finance, bored at home, sapped by stale marriages, with reticent or far-flung adult children and ill or dying friends, these women felt useful and appreciated. We formed a constellation of surrogates who likely should have been paying the dogs for therapy; it could have funded the entire shelter operation. We cried when dogs were euthanized but also when they were adopted; we had been seeking comfort in the constant and could barely deal with change. The term "shelter" seemed to apply as much to the humans as it did to the animals.

One's perspective on the number of animals it is appropriate to have within city limits changes when you're working at an animal shelter. To have no animals indicates that you're volunteering merely as a way of finding a pet to adopt, dabbling, putting you in a perennial state of searching, never to be taken seriously. Everyone waits for you to find your pet and then move on. Having merely one pet hints at a snootiness, as if your lifestyle is so refined, your abode so fastidious, your car so clean that only a single perfect creature will do. One dog or cat is more of an accessory. Most people who work with animals have at least two dogs, or two cats, or some combination thereof. But it is just as likely that a shelter worker or volunteer has four dogs and three cats and a rabbit, none of which get along, and a house set up like a kennel or boarding facility, with dog crates and baby gates, an upstairs/downstairs stratified dynamic, even going so far that spouses will sleep in separate rooms to accommodate the needs of the animals. These sacrifices and compromises are not seen as excessive but rather valiant.

After Sleater-Kinney ended, Corin threw herself into being a full-time mom, Janet immediately found other bands with which to play, and I, under the influence of the humane society culture, started bringing home dogs, fostering one after another, seeking a perfect fit. I already had one dog, but I went ahead and adopted a second. Now I found myself with my own menagerie.

There were four of them now, two cats and two dogs, one for each of my limbs; enough of them so that I could evenly disperse my worries and obsessions among them, worries that would have been too much for just one of them to bear. They were my family. We lived in my four-bedroom Craftsman home in northeast Portland, with a fake crow on the roof that I never stopped reminding people I didn't put up. It was a house big enough so that each of us could have had our own bedrooms if we'd wanted—and in a futile attempt to keep them off the furniture, there were in fact dog and cat beds everywhere but in the bathrooms. But instead, we all chose to sleep in mine. At night we vied for spots on the queen-size mattress, the cats my itchy neck warmers, one dog burrowing under the covers, the other in the crook of my knee. We were close enough that the exhalation of my breath made their ears twitch, that if one of them had fleas we all did, so near and entwined that I couldn't tell one whisker-filtered snore from another. Despite the daytime chases and cross-species pestering and a scuffling of paws, the occasional annoyed meow or impatient whine, in the bed at night we were all at peace. It was constricting, a fur coffin, but also a crib. If the fake crow were looking down on us, he would see a woman in her thirties, living alone, jobless and aimless, with animals to fill the space and to patch the holes.

Leaving the house became a series of meticulous rituals. The ones for my own benefit were easy: spend two minutes locating the keys, gather my wallet, lipstick, and gum, and place them in a cavernous bag, check my outfit in the entryway mirror, and leave. But the animals required much more.

Whenever I left, all I wanted to ensure was that I'd return to a space that was relatively the same as when I left. Sure, there would always be subtle changes: a couch pillow on the floor, the corner of it damp and freshly chewed, a shoe mysteriously moved from the entryway to beneath the coffee table, a rawhide half-eaten, releasing into the house that fake smoke flavor that's supposed to appeal to animals, as if dogs and cats, back in their days in the wild, barbecued their meats.

So, before I would leave, I prepared: I thought ahead, I predicted behaviors that could be set off by boredom, loneliness, or sheer instinct. Like my record collection transforming into a five-foot scratching post or my books becoming mealy tug toys. I minimized risk. Step one, the big one, was to tire the dogs out—as I'd learned in my training classes, 85 percent of behavioral problems stem from lack of exercise. So we went on runs until their tongues fell out the sides of their mouths in a collapse of pink. Once home, the dogs would crash for hours. All the other steps came later, right before I walked out the door: refresh the water bowls, leave out a few cat toys sprinkled with catnip, construct edible and impossible treats for the dogs that take them hours to eat, and finally, most important, rig the opening of the upstairs door with a piece of green garden twine, making a loop, leaving a gap just wide enough that the cats could slink through to the quiet and safety of upstairs, but too narrow for the big, boisterous dogs, who had a tendency to get into the cats' personal space.

Last, I would turn the radio on and say the words "Be good—I'll be back." I said this to no one animal in particular, but to all of them, and to myself, and because it's something I'd want to hear even if someone never intended to come home.

Hector, my first and oldest pet, was a sixteen-pound black cat with white details, a tuxedo cat with a chest broad and sturdy enough that I could lay my head upon it. He was a repressed and worried kitten when I got him at eight weeks of age, too thoughtful for silliness like string. I named him after the Greek warrior to instill in him a sense of empowerment and duty. He grew into the name and took on the other definition of "hector," which is "to bully," and when he was outdoors he made sure the neighborhood cats understood the concept of property lines. Hector brought me presents from the outside world: movie ticket stubs, old receipts, a parachute from a Fourth of July firework, and he once retrieved his own collar, lost weeks before. He announced the arrival of each gift with a tiny, high-pitched meow, comically disproportionate to his girth, like a football linebacker reading poetry. I'd had him since I was twenty-five; he had seen me through nearly a decade of living spaces, relationships, breakups, and tours; and when I called him "my best friend," I was only half joking.

Poor Lyle, my second pet and second cat, always a sidekick; gray and white, with half a mustache, an endless supply of eye gunk, an acrobatic vertical jump that rivaled a pro basketballer, and a penchant for announcing himself when he walked into a room, which would have been fine except that he was always walking into rooms. Lyle was constantly getting into scrapes. He survived a collision with a pickup truck and walked away without a single broken bone but with a tire tread across his face. He roamed around the neighborhood, crossed streets without looking both ways, tried to befriend a squirrel—he was stupidly, happily fearless, like a teenager on a dare. But he was also sensitive, particularly to my moods, absorbing my worry in his lithe little being. Whenever I moved cities or dwellings, Lyle would come down with gastritis. A plumbing disaster sent me into a rage when I bought my house in Portland, and immediately Lyle was back in the animal ER, not eating, vomiting up bile in dramatic, spastic heaves. The vets never could find the underlying cause of his illnesses. I figured that Lyle was just checking himself into rehab. He needed a little break. He always came back from his vet stays rehydrated, rested, and ready to deal with me anew.

Fortunately, both Lyle and I had Hector. Steady and unwavering. Worthy and tolerant of the Andrews Sisters–style songs I wrote about him, like the one called "Greatest Cuddler of All Time." Lyle and Hector spent much of their days locked in a yin-yang cuddle, Hector's fur matted and glossy from Lyle's diligent grooming.

When I realized that in fact I was the cause of Lyle's stress, with my anxieties and transferred hypochondria (it's not my fault that as a child when I drank a few extra glasses of orange juice my mom asked my dad if he thought I had diabetes, or that if I came home with more than one bruise on my leg she suggested I had leukemia), the most logical solution for Lyle was to find ways of creating a calmer household. I could have learned to play the pan flute or taken up yoga or meditation, but I got a dog instead. After all, I needed to spread my worry among more vessels, so that none would bear the brunt of it alone. Now I had a whole new species, one that demanded a lot more than my cats did.

This was Tobey, another boy, also another black and white, but bearded and wiry, some kind of pointer, and he quickly grew to sixty-five pounds of tightly coiled muscle. He mauled shoes and books; he stole rising pizza dough off the counter where it ballooned in his belly; he ate an entire bag of coffee beans; he side-tackled me at the river so hard it sent me to the ER. I was enchanted by his athleticism, even though all that made him agile made him potentially hurtful as well. It wasn't merely love, it was an adventure.

If we measured our affection toward others by how many nicknames we bestow upon them, our pets would be the most loved. Here's the etymological journey for the nicknames I have for Tobey: Tobito. Toblerone. T-Bone. T-bonics. Ta-T. Ta-Tobes. Tubby, for when he's gotten into the trash and gorged himself. Nicknames with origins based on appearance: Bearded Yum Yum, Handsome McHandsome, Fuzzy Face. Then this strange progression: Pooch. Poochers. Poocharoo. Poochacho. Pachune. Then, somehow, Pooch turned into Mooch, and so there had to be Moocharo. Muchacho. Manu, and most recently Man-nu-nu. All these monikers I say in voices more commonly echoed from the confines of straitjackets and padded walls. Anyone we truly love should come with their own dictionary.

Yet for all his strength and keen prey drive, Tobey was afraid of Hector, whining and doing a little tap dance in the hallway because the cat wouldn't let him pass. He shared armchairs with Lyle during TV shows and movies, jealous that the cats could sit higher, jump higher, and, most maddening, fit on my lap. We had struck a delicate but functional balance. A house with fourteen legs and four hearts. It should have been enough.

Here I was again without a family, my only identity a loner. A male loner is a hero of sorts, a rebel, an iconoclast, but the same is not true of a female loner. There is no virility in a woman's autonomy, there is only pity. I was floating. I had created my own abandonment.

At the Humane Society, after a year of resisting the charms of countless puppy litters and special-needs, blind, three-legged dogs without teeth, I fell in love with Joni Rose, a name better reserved for a twice-divorced aunt working a late shift in Reno than for a five-month old wrinkly-faced Shar-Pei mix with a circular bald patch on her nose. A fungus, they explained, or perhaps ringworm. I renamed her Olive to help bring out her cute side. She was my first female pet, a goofy brown nugget who communicated in a series of snorts, and in yawns so big they emitted a whistle. Unlike Tobey, she was easy to train, gentle and malleable. With Olive, I felt certain that I was done, complete. I had two pairs.

Yet now the balance felt tipped. I was both the center of attention and the odd number. I was suddenly in the middle, with the cats on one side and the dogs on the other. Olive, with her puppy curiosity, was unafraid of the cats, and Tobey's deference to them gave way to a new-found and sometimes alarming sense of empowerment.

Thus, the departure rituals, the precautionary measures in the house became more deliberate: an added cat door leading to the basement, a baby gate to keep the dogs out of certain rooms; the cats' realm became higher, more restricted. Safer, or so I thought.

One reason people get dogs is so there is always someone excited to see them when they get home. Whether I had been gone five hours or five minutes, Tobey and Olive's greeting was the same: effusive, sloppy, unabashed, a surprise party every time the key turned. It was my birthday, their birthday, Halloween and Christmas, confetti!

On that warm July night in 2007, I knew something was wrong when I returned home, opened the front door, and no one came to greet me. No wags, no slobber, no clumsy collision of noses to knees. There was an acrid smell in the house, an airlessness in the entryway. I walked farther in. I saw that the green twine preventing the dogs from getting through the upstairs door was broken, the stairway exposed. Olive and Tobey ran down; they were panting, wild-eyed, wet. I ran upstairs with the dogs at my heels. There were tufts of indistinguishable fur in the hallway, undercoat. I looked to the left into the music room.

Here is where all the air in the house had gone, to give this ugliness breath and a brutal force. There was the crumpled rug, more fur, and the still, black body of Hector. He lay next to my guitar, lifeless.

I ran downstairs. I dragged the dogs out into the backyard like intruders, like garbage. I picked up the phone. I called friends, inarticulate with shock. I tried to sink into the walls, I tried to climb them, I bore my way into the couch. My house could not hold me. A friend came to take the dogs away because if they stayed I said I would kill them. Yet I put together their dog food, carefully measuring out the servings in Tupperware containers, enough for a week, as if I were sending them away on vacation or to summer camp.

We wrapped Hector's body in a towel. I touched the tip of his tail, the white part that always looked like it had been dipped in paint. I held him. He was heavier than he'd ever been. We drove to the 24-hour animal hospital to have him cremated. It was the only time Hector didn't cry on the way to the vet.

I returned home to an empty house. Lyle had been outside the entire time.

I spent the next week sleeping downstairs on a lumpy futon mattress with Lyle, trying to get him to appreciate our time alone. He had all my attention. I brought out every cat toy, I put his food dish on the ground now that the dogs weren't around to steal from it, I bought him salmon-flavored snacks and played laser pointer until the batteries ran out. I wanted him to be sad, to miss Hector, to grieve, to comfort me. Mostly what I wanted was for Lyle to understand that for his own safety, he would be rehomed to a friend, that these would be our last days together, too. But like always Lyle just wanted to be outdoors; and it became clear to me that we weren't looking at this in the same way. Humans and animals rarely do.

There wasn't any blood. But when I could bring myself to return upstairs, it looked like a crime scene, the entire battle told in the deep, desperate scratches on the wood floor. It was clear that Hector had tried to hide under the bed, there had been a struggle in the hallway, and then, finally, in the music room, in that useless, sterile room that I kept as a mausoleum, a mourning I was ostensibly going to deal with when it was convenient, was a plain and sinister floor map upon which I could retrace every mistake I ever made. A body. A guitar.

Now, finally, I was sad. Here it was, that shadow that forms on your insides, a dark pooling, the grief. Everything I had was gone.

CHAPTER 21

HOME

Long ago I stopped focusing on performing for the sake of my family, but instead performed in spite of it, away from it, to get out. The bottomless urge I had to entertain as a child had sent me headstrong and hurling myself into rooms, hoping I'd arrive in time to delay or minimize the breakage. Cop, coach, clown. A one-girl Greek chorus there to protect, instruct, and delight. But there is no one I could really save but myself.

That's what I mean when I say Sleater-Kinney was my rescue and salvation. It was the first time I felt I could be vulnerable in my creativity in which the emotional and psychic stakes were neither futile nor self-annihilating. That unlit firecracker I carried around inside me in my youth, eager to ignite it at the slightest provocation, to detonate my whole being and fill the room in a glowing spectacle, found a home in music. My restlessness and unease was matched by my fellow miscreants—bandmates, collaborators, and audiences alike—but more crucially by a warmth and sustenance. In Sleater-Kinney, each song, each album, built an infrastructure, fresh skeletons. These, at last, were steady bones.

Now performing was no longer about trying to harness a cursory attention or to be a distraction. Sleater-Kinney allowed me to perform

both away from and into myself, to leave and to return, forget and discover. Within the world of the band there was a *me* and a *not* me, a fluc-
tuation of selves that I could reinvent along the flight between perches.
I could, at last, let go. For so long I had seen the lacking I'd been
handed as a deficit, my resulting anxiety and depression were ambient, a
tedious lassoing of air. But with Sleater-Kinney I stopped attempting to
contain or control the unknown. I could embrace the unnamed and the
in-between. I could engage in an unapologetic obliteration of the sacred.
Singularities had always been foreign to me, and where and who I came
from was rife with dualities, a mesh of conflicted and diluted selves
attempting to cohere, failing on account of an inarticulate denial. Fortunately, music granted me both an allowance of and a continual engagement with the ineffable. I also, for once, felt a part of something. The
inexplicable is its own form of freedom. Belonging is not a form of re-
striction. We can't name the feeling but we can sing along.

After we walked offstage at that final Sleater-Kinney show in 2006, we
went to the dressing room, we drank champagne, there were toasts and
cheers and hugs. Then we danced.

On the second floor of the Crystal Ballroom is a smaller venue and bar
called Lola's Room. While our friend DJed with '60s and '70s soul and
funk, New Wave and post-punk, we moved around the floor as a form of
relief, of revelation, of love. As is so often the case, the night turned out
to be less about the music we had played, and more about who we experienced the music with. When around three a.m. the club staff shut off the
sound system and turned on the lights, we stayed on the floor for nearly a
full five minutes stomping our feet and clapping our hands, still dancing.
We wanted more, to hear an echo, an encore of ourselves.

EPILOGUE

In 2011, Fred Armisen and I were at Corin and Lance's house. We were sitting on a lumpy behemoth of a couch that the Tucker-Bangs family called "mocha chenille," showing them an early cut of a *Portlandia* episode that featured their son, Marshall. Out of the blue, Corin asked if I thought Sleater-Kinney would ever play again. The answer was obvious.

We kept it a secret. Like when we'd traveled to the other side of the world in order to form our band. This time we created a continent of whispers. We wanted to protect the reassembly, wanted to make sure what we created didn't consist of anything broken, that it was three whole selves with the same hunger. Sleater-Kinney isn't something you can do half-assed or halfheartedly. We had to really want it, to need it. With no settled version of Sleater-Kinney, we also required the strength and willingness to push—we knew the entity that is this band would push right back. It always had. The secret was both frightening to keep and empowering to hold. The outcome uncertain, the stakes reset, the expectations high. For now, however, it was just us three, exactly how we wanted it.

The first time Janet and Corin and I played music together after six years apart was in Corin's basement. It was 2012. Surrounded by Lance's vertiginous and towering archives of magazines and records, we dusted off our own story. The goal on this day was to see if we could write together again, and in order to ease ourselves into the process, we had relearned old songs. In the first iteration of Sleater-Kinney it had always been a somewhat effortless process for me to recall how to play something when we'd reconvene for an album tour. Muscle memory kicked in and my fingers found the notes before my brain did. This was true six years later as well. What I didn't remember was how it feels to stand in a room while Corin Tucker sings. How her voice is the answer to so many of my questions, a validation, as if she knows the map of my veins. And I had forgotten the beastly avalanche that is Janet Weiss behind the kit, when our guitars are propelled by the cascading force of her. We ran through "Jumpers," and this time it was not about death, it was about being alive.

We would spend the next two years writing, telling few people about our plan.

In January 2015, Sleater-Kinney put out our first album in a decade. We called it *No Cities to Love*. Our first show of the tour was in the eastern Washington city of Spokane, where we'd never played before, a small, less-visited market. We wanted to begin on the fringes if we could, but that would not be the case. Journalists and photographers flew in. Fans came from as far away as Australia to be there.

As we always do about thirty minutes before show time, we cleared the backstage of friends and crew. Corin and I did vocal warm-ups while Janet drummed on a practice pad. On the outside I felt confident and happy, but internally I felt something close to disassociation. Our tour manager came to retrieve us and we walked to the side of the stage. The house lights went off and I wished I could sit in that blackness, that I could make everything and everyone disappear with a slow-moving blink. I was panicked that I had thrown myself into something I no longer knew how to do, no longer deserved to even be a part of. I was frightened I'd made a horrible mistake.

When I looked down, my feet were moving and I was headed stage right, to the place I've always stood in Sleater-Kinney. That was a start. I knew where to go and where to be. There was a thunderous greeting from the crowd; it was a "HELLO" so enormous I could climb inside. And I did. Tears stung my eyes. Corin started the first notes of "Price Tag," the opening track on the new album. Two bars later, Janet and I came in. I was in my body, joyous and unafraid. I was home.

ACKNOWLEDGMENTS

I could not have written this book without the wisdom, patience, and encouragement of my dear friend Chelsey Johnson. She read and oversaw this book through all of its stages, and I am immeasurably grateful for her guidance, friendship, and her continued faith in me. I would also like to thank my agent, Jud Laghi, who sought me out many years ago and whose confidence in me helped me find my way to this book's completion. Thanks to Geoffrey Kloske, my editor at Riverhead, for his assiduous feedback, supervision, and advice. Thank you to Caty Gordon for the diligence and fastidiousness. Thanks Megan Lynch for the early edits. Thank you to Corin Tucker and Janet Weiss, without whose friendship and loyalty I wouldn't have the strength to hold a pen, let alone a guitar. Thank you to my family: my father, sister, mother, Kurtis, Mike, Josh, Denise, Nat, and Gael. Thank you to my other family: Ben, Kathy, Max, Sophia, Moses, and Osa. Thank you to Fred Armisen, my friend and collaborator. Thank you to Liz Lambert for giving me a new room and city in which to write. Thanks to Bob Boilen, Robin Hilton, Stephen Thompson, and everyone at NPR

Music for allowing me to find my voice and wherein a handful of the ideas for this book percolated.

Thanks to my mentor and professor in sociolinguistics, Susan Fiksdal.

Thank you: Julie Butterfield; Bob Lawton; Chad Quierolo; Stephen O'Neil; Frances Gibson; Toni Gogin; Laura MacFarlane; Lance Bangs; Becca Albee; John Goodmanson; Dave Fridmann; Roger Moutenot; Donna Dresch; Mark Luecke; Kill Rock Stars; Matador Records; Sub Pop; Lever and Beam; the various crews, engineers, and technicians I've worked with in Sleater-Kinney; the musicians and bands I've been lucky enough to play shows with over the years; and the tremendous and inspiring S-K fans.

For their love and support I'd like to thank: Miranda July, Katie Harkin, Erin Smith, Patrick Stanton, Ryan Baldoz, Shannon Woodward, Tim Sarkes, Taylor Schilling, Ellen Page, Kim Gordon, Aimee Mann, Amy Poehler, Gaby Hoffmann, Jill Soloway, Wendy Donohue, Annie Clark, Lorne Michaels, Jonathan Krisel, Alice Mathias, Andrew Singer, Ashley Streicher, Jenn Streicher, Lena Dunham, Karey Dornetto, and Graham Wagner. I'm sure I've forgotten a few people, so I thank all of you now, anyone who inspired me to keep writing or keep thriving or keep trying. Lastly, thanks to the staff and volunteers at the Oregon Humane Society and to everyone at Riverhead/Penguin Random House.